The Dream Lives On

The Dream Lives On

Dorothy's Word

Edited by
JACOB W. ELIAS

RESOURCE *Publications* · Eugene, Oregon

THE DREAM LIVES ON
Dorothy's Word

Resource Publications
An Imprint of Wipf and Stock Publishers
199 W. 8th Ave., Suite 3
Eugene, OR 97401

www.wipfandstock.com

PAPERBACK ISBN: 978-1-6667-8367-4
HARDCOVER ISBN: 978-1-6667-8368-1
EBOOK ISBN: 978-1-6667-8369-8

VERSION NUMBER 08/23/23

Scripture quotations are from the New Revised Standard Version of the
Bible, copyright 1989 by the Division of Christian Education of the National Council of the Churches of Christ in the U.S.A.

Contents

Introduction

Dorothy Word, Dorothy's Word, and *The Dream Lives On*

DOROTHY WORD

AN AFRICAN AMERICAN WOMAN wrote the articles assembled in this volume. She was dreaming of a more hopeful future for her people. The compiler and editor is a white male Canadian-born citizen of the United States. My ancestors did not own slaves. However, I have increasingly become aware that I am a beneficiary of centuries of enslavement of people of African descent. The title *The Dream Lives On* puts the accent on a dream still struggling to become reality. Still casting doubt on the viability of that dream is the haunting nightmare of ongoing inequality, injustice and oppression.

It was during ten years (2001–2011) as pastors of Parkview Mennonite Church in Kokomo, Indiana, that my wife Lillian and I first became acquainted with Dorothy Word. We participated with her in the life and worship of the Parkview congregation. Photos from that period remind us of her active involvement with children in the congregational "Community Night" ministry. We joined her in various denominational activities, including the Damascus Road Anti-Racism project sponsored by Mennonite Central Committee. Our interaction with her came to an end during our fourth year as Parkview pastors. In 2004 Dorothy moved back to her home town, Fort Wayne, to be closer to her family.

Eight years later Lillian and I reconnected with Dorothy. We moved to Goshen in 2012, about a year into our retirement. We soon discovered that Dorothy was a resident in an assisted living apartment at nearby Waterford Crossing. It was immediately apparent to us that she had experienced significant cognitive decline during the intervening years. It was not obvious to us why she had moved to Goshen, and Dorothy was no longer able to tell us.

Shortly after resuming our relationship with Dorothy I was asked to assume the power of attorney to assist her in making healthcare and financial decisions. Apparently no one in her family was able or willing to take this responsibility.

We moved her from Waterford Crossing to Golden Living, Elkhart, in 2015, and then in 2018 to Green House Village of Goshen (now called The Laurels of Goshen). For each of these moves Lillian and I sorted through her already downsized material possessions, storing some and donating others. We accompanied her for almost eight years of her journey ever deeper into dementia. In many ways Lillian and I became surrogate members of Dorothy's family. At consultations to review care plans she was identified as "your loved one." We typically visited her on a weekly basis. And we communicated by letters, phone calls and emails with her friends and family members, using Dorothy's contact list, which I expanded and updated over the years. After her death on November 1, 2020, we shared the news with family and friends by making phone calls and sending emails. We also made final arrangements, based on guidelines that she had put in writing when she contracted for a prepaid funeral plan with Ellis Funeral Home in Fort Wayne. On November 6, 2020, Lillian and I led a private family graveside service in the Covington Memorial Gardens, Fort Wayne.

Another task normally performed by someone from the family of the deceased is to submit an obituary to newspapers. Dorothy had written a provisional obituary, which I updated and submitted to newspapers in Evansville, Kokomo, and Fort Wayne, the communities where she had lived. I include Dorothy's first draft of her obituary here. It is Dorothy's life story in her own words, the only personal summary of her life to which we have access. She entitled it "The Final Call." Above the title, in her handwriting, is the instruction: "Put in Newspaper."

> Dorothy Phinezy Word passed away . . . She was born in Fort Wayne, Indiana on February 12, 1938. She is survived by a son and a host of nephews and nieces (her sisters?) She was active in United Methodist organizations, Church Women United, Kokomo, Indiana and was a pioneer member of the Fairhaven Mennonite Church in Fort Wayne.
>
> She attended Fort Wayne Community Schools and graduated from Central High School in 1956. She earned a Bachelor's Degree in Education from Indiana Wesleyan University (formerly Marion College) and a Master's Degree in Education from Indiana University in Bloomington, IN.
>
> In the 1960s she returned to Fort Wayne and taught at Harmar and Study Elementary Schools and Adult Evening Class at McCulloch Elementary School. She taught Head Start in Nashville, Tennessee, and later taught in the New Castle School System and the Blue River Valley School System which included the Migrant Mexican programs, Special Education, L.D. classes and Second Grade.
>
> She ended her teaching career in the Evansville-Vanderburgh School Corporation in June 1995. After retirement she tutored students and taught English as a Second Language (ESL). Also she became a freelance newspaper writer for *Our Times* in Evansville, *Kokomo Tribune* in Kokomo, IN, and *Frost Illustrated* in Fort Wayne.

Dorothy makes several references to her participation in United Methodist organizations. Not mentioned in this brief bio are several affiliations that I would have expected, given what we had learned about her life journey. Dorothy mentions that she was a pioneer member of Fairhaven Mennonite Church, but there are no other references to her Mennonite connections. As already mentioned, we met her when she was active in Parkview Mennonite Church. We have heard from people in the Fairview Mennonite Church, Fort Wayne, that she became involved there again after she moved back to Fort Wayne. Among her papers was a Certificate of Baptism, dated November 7, 1954. Bishop S. J. Miller officiated at the baptism. Congregational memory of Dorothy as a child testifies that she first became involved in this emerging church when she was invited to attend their Vacation Bible School.

The fact that Dorothy includes references to her participation in United Methodist congregations and organizations aligns with what we knew about her. She seems to have felt at home in both denominations. Sometimes she surprised us by comments that reflected what she held as Mennonite values. I share an anecdote from our experience with her when she was in Assisted Living at Waterford Crossing. We accompanied her to a party. When she saw a beverage table she did not want to enter the room. "I don't drink," she explained. "I'm a Mennonite." When we assured her that no alcohol was being served she agreed to join the party.

During the process of working on this anthology I often yearned for more information about Dorothy's life. Our contact with her when she was still in good health was limited to almost four years. There are questions I wish now that I would have asked her about her life, her family, and her acquaintance with her ancestral story.

DOROTHY'S WORD

Dorothy ends the draft of her obituary by noting that she wrote newspaper columns. Beginning in 1995 she was a guest columnist for local newspapers in the cities where she lived. Her first columns appeared in 1995–96 in the *Our Times* newspaper in Evansville, which was billed as "the tri-states only African American Newspaper since 1983." She wrote around 50 brief articles for *Our Times* under the title "Kuumba Corner of Black History" before she retired in Kokomo, IN. It was during her years in Kokomo (1996 to 2004) that she wrote regular columns for the *Kokomo Tribune*. Forty of the 41 articles in this collection were published in the *Kokomo Tribune*. In 2004 when Dorothy moved to Fort Wayne, IN she started writing for *Frost Illustrated*, a weekly newspaper that described itself as "featuring news and views of African Americans." In her collection of writings from that era I found six brief articles, some apparently submitted but not published. She wrote under the caption, "Dorothy's Word."

How many articles did Dorothy write? The articles in this volume are mostly what she had personally stored. Research in the archives of the three newspapers that published her articles would be needed to determine the number and to establish the dates when they were published. According to a personal note appended to some articles that she passed on to a friend, Dorothy says, "I hope you will enjoy my articles. They span from 1996 to 2007." Joe Springer, retired archivist at Goshen College, conducted a search of the *Kokomo Tribune* articles and found 106 entries over the period, January 1, 1996 to December 31, 2004.

I distinctly recall one of our visits with Dorothy when she was still living in Waterford Crossing. She pointed toward a two-drawer filing cabinet and gestured for me to open the top drawer. There I found a pile of her newspaper columns. They had been clipped and thrown into this filing cabinet drawer. In many cases, unfortunately, the date of publication had been cut off. Some were tucked into 8½" by 11" brown envelopes on which she had recorded some titles and dates. Dorothy was disciplined and organized in some areas of her professional and personal life, but her filing practices were haphazard. Her dementia had robbed her of the ability to express herself coherently about what she wanted me to do with these writings. When she moved out of Waterford Crossing we stored these newspaper columns in our home. After Dorothy died we knew that we would need to decide what to do with them.

I consulted with Jason Kauffman, archivist for Mennonite Church USA, who agreed to house Dorothy's writings in the MCUSA Archives in Elkhart, Indiana. Jason also arranged to digitize this collection to enable remote access.

The question soon arose: Should these articles be published? I explored this possibility with the Institute of Mennonite Studies at Anabaptist Mennonite Biblical Seminary and was encouraged to submit a proposal. There was strong interest but in the end they determined that, given their primary mission and current priorities, they could not include this volume in their publishing schedule.

An important factor when considering publication was, for what audience? Would newspaper columns initially crafted for local newspapers in small cities in the American Midwest generate sufficient interest to warrant being published as an anthology?

In the end I decided that I needed to pursue publication. At a personal level I feel compelled to do something that will help this African American woman, a Mennonite with United Methodist connections, a creative teacher and activist and writer, to be remembered. At the societal level I sense that Dorothy's voice needs to be heard. I recognize that Dorothy did not enjoy name recognition as a noted scholar or politician or journalist. However, I am persuaded that the dream for justice and authentic inclusion that she articulated in her writings can make a significant contribution in undoing racism beyond her lifetime. "On the ground" perspectives of people in the back rows of the arena of public awareness have the potential to cultivate intercultural competence. In the chronically polarizing political discourse of 21st century America such competence is sorely needed for negotiating relationships in the landscape of ongoing racial ethnic conflict.

Dorothy's newspaper columns are of interest in the circle of her family and friends, but they also have broader relevance in the struggle between white supremacist impulses and "Black Lives Matter" activism. The topics that she addresses in her columns include family life, education, race relations, Black heritage, women's roles, and a variety of justice issues faced by people of color in America. Dorothy frequently highlights the work of African American scientists, athletes, musicians, educators, soldiers and inventors whose contributions during their lifetimes were inadequately acknowledged or even blatantly dismissed.

Readers of Dorothy's articles rarely get glimpses into her personal journey, family life, teaching career, and relationships. Her newspaper columns consistently expose political and societal ills as experienced by people whose racial identity and ancestral history she shared, but her own painful personal experiences are largely

6

left unaddressed. When I try to understand the relative absence of autobiographical reflections in her writings I am reminded that significant trauma in her personal life erupted during the approximately eight years between her return to Fort Wayne in 2004 and her move into an assisted living unit in Goshen in 2012. It was during that time that she began to deal with memory loss and the confusion and anger associated with her descent into the darkness of dementia. Lillian and I have heard some anecdotes about her life during those years but we have not tried to reconstruct what all was happening to her. In her halting efforts to communicate her memories and describe her feelings we gained some impressions but rarely learned details about that period of her life.

THE DREAM LIVES ON

Dorothy did not create syndicated columns for release to a number of newspapers. She wrote as a guest columnist for local newspapers. Her columns were apparently written when she had time or inspiration to do so, and they were published when there was space for them to be included. The topics Dorothy addressed usually reflected her own interests or the results of her research, but she also wrote on themes suitable for current seasons or family celebrations.

When I was considering how to organize this collection I soon realized that a chronological approach would not be feasible. The challenge of introducing her articles with reference to current events, locally, nationally or globally, was more onerous than I was willing to attempt. And, as already indicated, we have minimal awareness of the deeper dimensions of Dorothy's life. I settled on a thematic approach instead.

In the following pages the reader will find Dorothy's columns organized along five themes, briefly noted: village, family, school, heritage, and dream. These categories obviously overlap but I use them to help provide structure. A chapter is devoted to each of these themes.

Most chapters open with testimonials written by some of Dorothy's friends and acquaintances. Some of our memories of

Dorothy appear as well. I also provide an overview of the overarching theme of the articles incorporated into each chapter. What follow are brief transitional statements introducing each of the articles. Dorothy speaks for herself in these articles, so I borrow the caption that Dorothy used in her final columns: "Dorothy's Word."

At the end of each chapter I imagine myself entering into conversation with Dorothy or her intended readers. I entitle this section, "I ponder…" I reflect on my village, family, school, heritage and dream, and invite readers to engage in individual reflection on these themes. As an African American woman, who became an accomplished elementary school teacher and later a newspaper columnist, Dorothy was often an advocate for the marginalized. As a person raised in relative privilege, I sit down, as it were, with this woman and other conversation partners to wrestle with our respective histories, experiences and perspectives. I am hopeful that my readers will feel invited into collaborative efforts to seek for and work toward a hopeful future.

Before beginning the process of interacting with "Dorothy's Word" I need to offer a personal comment. Dorothy is not among us to defend herself or correct my interpretations of her writings. "Jacob's word" has unavoidably taken on some level of prominence in this project, even though the primary intent has been to allow "Dorothy's Word" to be heard.

I am aware that my judgments led to choices about which columns to include. There are many other articles that could have been incorporated. I chose to feature articles that she passed on to me, most of which were published in the *Kokomo Tribune*. I organized the chapters in a sequence that seemed to me to be representative of her work. However, it is also evident to me that my chosen categories were imposed on what she wrote.

During my career as Professor of New Testament at Anabaptist Mennonite Biblical Seminary, Elkhart, IN (1977 to 2008) I always sought to interpret biblical literature from within a big picture. My primary role during the last half of my 31 year tenure was to teach courses on the writings of the apostle Paul. I introduced my students to the process of reading the letters of the apostle

Paul from within a dynamic narrative framework. The faith community is the Village, an interdependent network of individuals, families, and congregations with an overarching story (heritage) that embodies the dream of a hopeful and fruitful future. Some readers of this anthology of Dorothy's writings may be familiar with my book, *Remember the Future: The Pastoral Theology of Paul the Apostle* (Herald Press, 2006). I did not intentionally set out to place Dorothy's writings within a comparable overarching narrative that shaped the values and life direction of her ethnic and faith community, but I sense similarities.

Dorothy viewed herself as a participant in communities shaped by the historical heritage of the African American people. Her longing was that this heritage would increasingly enable these communities to participate in the realization of the dream eloquently shared by Martin Luther King Jr in his "I have a dream" speech shortly before his death.

The title of this book highlights this dream. The dreamer was killed, but the dream lives on. Dorothy was a participant in the race for justice and equality, but she also takes on the role of a cheerleader encouraging others to remain resilient in the quest for the realization of this dream.

1

Village

ONE OF DOROTHY'S EARLY columns describes the formative role of "the Village" in shaping the identity of a child. Before presenting a transcript of this column, we'll hear from one of her childhood friends, Rosalyn Ledyard, who describes the Village that helped to form Dorothy as a child and teenager. Apparently Dorothy also benefited from the same support network when, as an adult, she needed a listening ear and some non-judgmental counsel to help her deal with personal challenges in her marriage.

> My family of origin, Cletus and Luella Grieser and their children (I am the oldest) chose to attend Fairview Mennonite Church in Fort Wayne to establish a congregation in a multiracial neighborhood in 1954. Dorothy and I met as teens; I was 14 and she was 16. This relationship continued until I married and moved out of state and she was at Goshen College.
>
> Dorothy came to our home near Leo, Indiana many weekends and stayed with our big family. She was part of the family for years and often visiting our Mother after Dorothy married. Mother had a listening ear and tried to

understand from her and Calvin's perspective when their marriage was failing.

Our family ties were broken for a period but were healed after years of separation. We thanked God when the return of relationships began again and Mother and my sister could again relate to her. (Rosalyn M. Ledyard, via email, sent on July 2, 2022)

On several occasions in the course of her journey from teaching to retirement Dorothy benefited from practical helpfulness offered by the Village. She kept a daily journal of her move from Evansville to Kokomo in October 1996. Members of Parkview Mennonite Church were actively involved in helping her with this move. In 2004 she decided to leave Kokomo and return to Fort Wayne. Again the Parkview congregation went into action. Dorothy chronicled that move in her letter of gratitude to the church for their help:

A "Mennonite Caravan" got me here, October 30, afternoon. Grace and I were in the lead car, Jake in the rental truck, Lillian in their van, Bryce next, Bob driving my car. Milo, Clayton, Jake Graber and Eleanor were "left behind." (What would President Bush think about that?) "No adult left behind."

Fort Wayne Mennonites helped us unload. There were four of them plus my niece. They also brought snacks and bottled water.

Presently I am attending Fairhaven Mennonite Church where I was baptized 50 years ago.

I think of you often. Love and prayers, Dorothy W.

About eight years after relocating in Fort Wayne, Dorothy was guided in the decision to join an assisted living community at Waterford Crossing in Goshen. She was beginning to show symptoms of dementia. Later she moved to Golden Living in Elkhart, where she received care for several years. Eventually in 2018 in my exercise of durable power of attorney for healthcare decisions we transferred her to a senior care home where she lived her last years. It had a name that would have rung a bell for Dorothy when her cognitive abilities were still strong: Greenhouse Village of Goshen.

She felt embraced by this Village when she was an adult in her 80s struggling with dementia. Green House Village featured four separate houses, each with the capacity to accommodate twelve elders. Dorothy's place was called Strawberry Field. It had a welcoming family feel. Common space for meals, recreational activities, and social interaction cultivated a warm and inviting ambience of hospitality and love.

I share one more brief anecdotal comment, to illustrate the fact that Dorothy was the beneficiary of a caring Village. Dorothy was especially receptive toward children. Maynard Kurtz, whose wife Hilda was an elder receiving memory care in the same facility, shares how their granddaughter, Elisa, interacted with the elders, becoming an active partner in this caring network. Among other things, Elisa read children's books to Dorothy. I share a brief testimonial written by her grandpa Maynard:

> When Elisa, at age 10 and 11, came to Strawberry Field to visit her grandma, she took keen interest in the other residents as well. She intentionally sought out Dorothy, and the others, and spent time with her. Traditional conversation could not happen but there was positive interaction. Elisa offered hope and encouragement. A lot of love and appreciation flowed in both directions. To me, it appeared that Elisa brought a positive, pastoral presence.

In a word, Dorothy was sustained by the Greenhouse Village, a supportive web of relationships. To Dorothy's great delight this included the active participation of children.

DOROTHY'S WORD

1.1

An article published on December 6, 1996 as part of the series, "Kuumba Korner of Black History" in the Evansville *Our Times* newspaper is a forthright declaration of the need for community. Dorothy wrote a letter addressed to "Virginia". . . likely an anonymous name of a child:

Virginia, remember when the scoffers and the naysayers tried to crush your world? Your father wrote to a newspaper editor who assured you: "Yes, Virginia, there is a Santa Claus." Well, they're back!! This time they are attacking a much revered wisdom-laden African Proverb. But, we won't back down either. "Yes, Virginia, it takes a Village."

The Village is all about family. The Village is family values best exemplified by the fabric of the Black Church whose threads twined African American families from time immemorial. The Village embraces the family, shores up and gives it that extra boost that ALL families need at one time or another. The Village is that multifarious family of supportive community.

The Village is extensive and inclusive, encircling domestics and doctors; beauticians, bankers; teachers and TV hosts; singers and scientists; preachers and politicians; authors and actors, and all African Americans striving toward the 21st century.

African Americans were birthed, nurtured, role-modeled, encouraged, admonished, supported and applauded in the Village and necessarily sent forth into the non-village world where those in the nuclei-family bubble and those who thrive in isolationism and disconnectedness brazenly proclaim that the Village never accomplished the positive actions mentioned above. They also erroneously clamor that the Village is welfare and big government. These scoffers and naysayers are on the wrong Bridge, are on the wrong Track and are just plain wrong!!

Taking this honorable African Proverb and misconstruing it and degrading it into a political pawn is unconscionable.

Dorothy highlights the ways in which this African proverb became reality in the Black church and the African American community at large. She also appears to be echoing themes from the 1996 book *It Takes a Village* by Hilary Rodham Clinton. Reaction to that book, especially in conservative political circles, closely paralleled the views that Dorothy vigorously refutes in this column. She laments what she calls the "isolationism and disconnectedness" in so much public discourse. And she applauds the role of the Village as an interdependent network of people who support each other and provide an environment that nurtures children.

1.2

Dorothy's later columns deal less directly (and less confrontationally) with the rich cross-cultural connectedness that has the potential to shape life for people of all generations and backgrounds. One of her articles tells the story of the emergence of Patchwork Central in Evansville, Indiana, which sought to improve race relations, specifically by creating an inclusive multi-cultural environment.

A Community Group in Evansville is an Example to All (*Kokomo Tribune*, October 18, 1997)

In June President Clinton appointed Dr. John Hope Franklin, an Afro-American, to head up a special panel to examine race relations in America.

Dr. Franklin is a researcher, scholar, professor emeritus, historian and author and eminently qualified for this daunting task assigned to him.

As an historian and author, Franklin has written extensively about the histories of black people and white people. He is keenly aware that a 300 year old legacy of slavery and its divisive ideologies "can't change overnight."

I know that there are people who strongly resist change; people who are comfortable with the status quo of old negative stereotypes; people who discredited neighborhood activities across race and culture; and people who demean the current attempts at a national discussion on race.

But, already, Franklin's seven member board has heard reports from communities working toward racial harmony.

Franklin cites a group of blacks and Hispanics in his hometown of Durham, N.C., as one of the many groups "doing something to make their little corner of the world more genteel, more friendly, more upstanding."

Patchwork Central, Inc. of Evansville, Indiana has been working for the past years in "their little corner of the world" to improve race relations and to foster racial harmony.

In 1977, three white couples, (the Kimbroughs, Amersons, Doyles), who were good friends, shared a common desire. "We were hippies with a dream of working in the inner city," Nelia Kimbrough said.

Their dream became Patchwork Central. They not only worked in the inner city, they intentionally lived there, raised their kids there and sent their kids to school there.

In 1978, when school officials planned to close the neighborhood integrated inner city school, the Patchwork Central founders, their staff and volunteers organized the neighborhood to stop that plan. The school was razed, but a new school was built on that same site. When I moved to Evansville in 1983, my son Bryce had a brand new school to attend, less than three blocks from our home, thanks to Patchwork Central and the united neighborhood.

There were other successes: After-school Programs of tutoring, music and art; a Neighborhood Economic Development Center for people wanting to start small businesses; a neighborhood dental program; the Back Alley Bakery; and the Garden Patch.

After my retirement, I was able to volunteer full-time at Patchwork Central. I worked mainly in an after-school program. At Patchwork, I observed first-hand that people of color and whites were working together on a common goal of making "their little corner of the world more genteel, more friendly, more upstanding."

Patchwork Central celebrated its 20th Anniversary this past July and has demonstrated for two decades that where there's will, there's a way.

1.3

Dorothy urges mutual acceptance of people of diverse ethnic and cultural backgrounds. She celebrates the rich variety of languages spoken by recent immigrants who are also learning to speak English. And she refutes the presumption that immigrants are not authentic Americans.

> **An American is an American** (*Kokomo Tribune*, September 17, 2002)
>
> Thomas Hood's poem "I Remember, I Remember" is very nostalgic. It begins, "I remember, I remember the house where I was born." I have less nostalgia than the poet but I remember, I remember the house where I was raised in Fort Wayne. I remember the unpaved, dead-end street. I remember the neighbors. I remember the Mexican family that lived cater-corner across the street from our house. I remember they moved away before I really got to know them.
>
> On Catalpa Street, a few blocks away, I remember there were four Mexicans I did get to know—Hope, Mary, Virginia and their brother Alex. We girls sometimes walked to school together. Of course, Alex wouldn't walk with us, but I remember that in my fourth-grade opinion, Alex was "the finest thing that ever walked in shoe leather." (Translation: He was the "essence of cool.")
>
> Back on my street, Strathmore Street, another Mexican family moved into the house vacated by the "short-stay" family. Ybarra was the name of the new family. Their youngest member was a girl about my age named Licha. She and I became friends for life. After high school we went our separate ways but we still kept in touch—from those teenage years to this present time.
>
> When we do get together English is spoken. Licha's sister, her brother, sisters-in-law, nieces and nephew also speak English. Licha's mother and father, of course, spoke Spanish. Licha is a bilingual Mexican-American who speaks English and Spanish. Her daughter understands Spanish but speaks English. Granddaughter is an "English only" person. This is a common generational pattern.

Pastor Richard Solberg, a Lutheran minister in Rogers, Arkansas believes this generational language pattern is the same for ALL Americans. "My grandmother never learned to speak English," he said. His grandmother came to America from Norway. His mother and her sister immigrated too. Solberg's parents were bilingual but Solberg "never understood a word of what my grandmother said!"

It is not unusual for second, third and fourth generation Americans to speak English most of the time or all of the time. Mexican-Americans follow that same generational language pattern. That pattern is as American as apple pie and tacos!

I am amazed at the number of people in Kokomo who believe Mexican-Americans are undocumented migrant workers. I am amused at their disbelief that Mexican-Americans can and do speak "good" English. One Kokomo person informed me that, "They speak Mexican."

When I taught school in Fort Wayne, 99 percent of my Mexican-American students came from English-speaking homes.

There is a poster with a tongue-in-cheek message printed on it: "If you speak three or more languages, you are multilingual. If you speak two languages, you are bilingual. If you speak only one language, you are an American!"

(Well, not exactly.)

You're an American if you were born in America: "born in the U.S.A." You're an American whether you can speak one language or many. And if all those signs that went up after September 11—United We Stand—-really mean "united" then no group of Americans should be mislabeled, ignored, or left behind.

An American is an American is an American. (No translation needed.)

1.4

Sharing food in a cross-cultural setting is one expression of the global character of the interconnected Village. In an article that was apparently written in November 2002 Dorothy tells about a Thanksgiving meal featuring people from around the world and the food they contributed for their mutual enjoyment. This meal reminds her of the United Nations as a global Village of nations working together for the benefit of all people.

> **A recipe or two to bring us closer together** (*Kokomo Tribune*, Thanksgiving 2002)
>
> Thanksgiving Day 2001 was the day of a global gathering at hostess Huey Ching's home in Kokomo. I knew I was in for a "cuisine treat." And the sights, smells and tastes from around the world confirmed that diversity and inclusion would be the order of the day.
>
> I wasn't the only person aware of the "global reach" we represented at the table as we talked, laughed and partook of a delicious, copious meal. "This is a United Nations Thanksgiving," observed Marcilina who came from the Philippines. If we had a roll call it would have looked like this: African-American, European-Americans, Chinese, Indian (from India), Filipinos, South American, Vietnamese.
>
> Nhi, a Vietnamese, consented to be my unpaid secretary and wrote down the international menu. Not a good time or place to count calories.
>
> Main dishes: Chinese roasted pork. Turkey with Chinese seasonings and shiitake mushrooms. Stuffing (cornbread with raisins, nuts, apples). Mashed potatoes with Mexican cheese and butter. Philippine stew/Menodo (potatoes, peas, garbanzos, raisins, sweet/colored peppers, pork, liver pate, spices). Gravy.
>
> Vegetarian dishes: Spinach lasagna, Indian curry (potatoes, sweet potatoes, yellow squash, coconut milk, spices). Sautéed mushrooms. Steamed asparagus. Veggie tray and dip. Rice, corn, peas. Chinese mock roasted duck. French bread and bruschetta, roma tomatoes, basil, olive oil, garlic, salt.

Desserts: Chinese jello (seaweed, gelatin, red beans, pineapple chunks). Vietnamese cassava cake (banb khoai mi, cassava/yucca root, cornstarch, mung beans, coconut milk, sugar, butter). Peruvian panehonne bread (sweet). Fruit bowl (cantaloupe, honeydew, grapes). Pies—pumpkin, cherry, Dutch apple crunch.

Snacks: Eggrolls, cheese sticks, taquitos, shrimp cocktails, cheese balls.

I am convinced if we ALL sat down together with open minds (and hearts) and talked and laughed and ate together, the world would be a better place and PEACE would have a "fighting chance."

In the summer of 1995 I attended a very interesting meeting in Indianapolis and learned a lot about the United Nations in an in-depth 4-day study session. I learned about the U.N.'s failure and successes. And there were successes like the World Health Organization (WHO), a specialized agency of the U.N. dealing with global health problems.

Years ago, the WHO successfully eradicated smallpox from the face of the earth! The Universal Postal Union (UPU) is the U.N. agency that made international mail delivery possible. UNICEF, the United Nations Children's Fund offers an alternative activity for children who want to celebrate Halloween in a non-traditional way. The list goes on.

Add to that list the U.N. Weapons Inspection Resolution Mission—successful—at least for now. Add to that list last year's Nobel Peace Prize winner, U.N. Secretary General Kofi Annan. Imagine his massive job of trying to deal with 191 countries, each with its own agenda and issues.

The U.N. is more "American" than most of us realize. Did you know that many U.S. Protestant churches were involved with the conception and birth of the United Nations? Did you know that the language in the U.N. Preamble and the U.N. Charter was greatly influenced by Protestant Church leaders? Did you know that there is a United Nations hymn?

The United Nations Hymn was one of the handouts I received in my United Nations class in Indianapolis in

1995. The author is unknown but the tune is from Ludwig van Beethoven's "Ode to Joy" better known to many church folks as "Joyful, Joyful, We Adore Thee."

The words of the United Nations Hymn are as relevant today as they were when the author wrote them, maybe even more so right now as we await the Weapons Inspection outcome.

The United Nations Hymn:
Thou whose breathing fills our bodies,
Thou whose pulse the worlds obey.
Tune our mind to heed Thy rhythm
Known along the starry way.
Swing the nations to Thy measure,
Bid men's hatreds turn to song;
Fill us, thrill us with Thy music,
End earth's bitterness and wrong.
Thou whose order rules the atom,
Thou whose law propels the sea,
Bring, oh bring, Thy warring peoples
Close within Thy harmony.
God of beauty, heal our madness,
God of love, our battles end.
Show the unity that binds us,
Foe to foe, friend to friend.[1]

1.5

In November 2003 Dorothy's mind navigates from a feast where abundant food is shared to the realization that the tragedy of global hunger persists. However, she also celebrates efforts, both local and international, to help provide food for the hungry.

Hunger Problem is Getting Worse (*Kokomo Tribune*, November 4, 2003)

Oscar Hammerstein wrote the lyrics. Richard Rodgers wrote the music. But Julie Andrews made the song

---

1. The author of this hymn text was the poet Angela Morgan (1875–1957). Information about how or when these lyrics came to be acknowledged as a United Nations Hymn has not become available to me.

come alive in the movie "The Sound of Music" when she sang about some simple pleasures. Bright copper kettles, crisp apple strudels, doorbells, sleigh-bells and schnitzels with noodles. "These are a few of my favorite things," she sang.

On another occasion, a happy, hungry grandchild sang the second verse of that old traditional song that named two of his tasty favorites. "Over the river and through the wood, now grandmother's cap I spy! Hurrah for the fun! Is the pudding done? Hurrah for the apple pie!"

Singing about one's favorite things or making a list of one's favorite things point to the fast approaching special season—Thanksgiving, Christmas.

Then comes the New Year with all those resolutions about diets and pounds to shed. But that's for later! In the meantime, seasonal favorite things to eat are a high priority. Things like turkey and dressing, maybe a baked ham, pumpkin pie with or without whipped topping, homemade and store-bought cranberry sauce; the list goes on.

Ohioan, retired school principal, Bruce Stambaugh writes about "our bounty" and how easy it is to take our bounty, our abundance of food for granted. Stambaugh writes in *Rejoice!* a paperback devotional that, "Research shows if you have food left over at the end of a day, you are in the richest 25 percent of the world's population." Our leftovers would/could feed many of the world's hungry people, says Stambaugh.

At this time of year most people are keenly aware of the hunger problem. And many people are motivated to support activities aimed at feeding the hungry. I admire the Kokomo Rescue Mission policy of feeding the needy and not worrying about who might be greedy.

There are some local people who believe feeding the hungry should be confined to Kokomo and perhaps Howard County. On Sunday, October 12, about 70 people with an opposite view, who believe hunger has no borders, took part in a Heifer Project Walk to raise "money for the hungry of the world."

World Ark magazine is a Heifer International publication that explains the Heifer mission of "commitment to helping hungry families feed themselves and care for the earth" regardless of race, religion or belief. "Help goes to those in need from those who are able to give."

Parkview Mennonite Church of Kokomo is a small church within a small denomination. Nevertheless, Parkview Church and Mennonites in USA and Canada, like Heifer International, have "a global reach" spanning the globe.

This past August, Parkview Mennonite Church along with other Indiana and Michigan Mennonites combined their efforts and launched a "Penny Power" project, a fund-raiser to finance self-help projects around the world.

Penny Power is powerful. "Five pennies will buy enough sugar and salt for a rehydration solution to save one child from death in a Nigerian health clinic. Sixty pennies provide seed samples for one farmer in Haiti. One hundred fifty pennies buy a pair of ducklings for a poor family in Laos. Four hundred pennies provide a pair of ducks for a child in Indonesia. Eight hundred pennies buy a garden hand tool for refugees in Ethiopia. Two thousand pennies provide chickens for one family in the West Bank. Also, two thousand pennies allow a family in Vietnam to buy materials to set up five beehives. Six thousand pennies will stock one pond with fingerlings in Laos."

The world seems to be unevenly divided between the "feast" and "famine" populations. There are reasons for that unevenness. One reason is the cycle of droughts causing crop failures in poor countries. They certainly can't control the weather. Can any country?

Judy Kading, a church and community worker for the United Methodist Church, noted another reason. "About 80 percent of the world's people must share 15% of the world's resources left to them by the First World countries."

The U.S., one of those First World countries, does send food aid to some starving countries, and has many ways and resources to deal with hunger in America.

Many U.S. churches and other U.S. groups help the hungry, here and abroad on a daily basis. But there is still more that needs to be done. The hunger problem will not go away. It is here to stay and unfortunately it is getting worse.

1.6

Among women in their 80s Dorothy highlights several whose active life style focuses on voluntarism. Their involvements refresh the lives of people around them. The image of a flowing stream helps Dorothy to express her gratitude for their exemplary contribution to the welfare of others.

Ladies in their Eighties Help to Keep Life's River Alive
(*Kokomo Tribune*, June 3, 1999)

Tricia Goyer of Montana writes, "Behind my house is a river that flows crystal clear. Also behind my house, a little further inland, is a stagnant pond. Unlike the river, the pond builds up slime and muck because it does not flow. Its stillness makes the water foul and undrinkable. But the river's constant movement has kept its water fresh."

Patricia Goyer uses the river and the pond as an analogy to life itself. Choose not to "flow" and become "stagnant" or choose to "flow" like the river and refresh others and yourself as well.

Because of their long-life-experiences, the older generation is the most qualified to be "out-flowing," to "refresh" those around them. I am thinking specifically of some older women whose lifestyles are refreshing like "the river's constant movement." I call these women Ladies in the Eighties, not the 1980s but women 80 years old and older!

Singer-actress Lena Horne will be 82 years old on June 17. She is a Lady in the Eighties who continues her singing career and enjoys it more than ever before. Her musicians are glad she's still around. Her audiences are thrilled. The music critics are amazed.

Nearly no one realized that Miss Horne was an actress in her younger days because her speaking parts were cut from the movies to appease southern movie goers.

Lena Horne disliked Hollywood (MGM) and California because she was never free to be herself, and she was denied movie roles she desperately wanted. Next, she was blacklisted. That means she was completely barred from making movies or TV appearance for seven years.

Today, this grandmother and great grandmother is happy to be "free at last" from the past, and happy to be singing and interacting with her many devoted fans. Lena Horne: The Lady and her Music.

Rosa Parks was 86 years old in February. Her influence on America and Americans seems as fresh today as it was in 1955 when she refused to give up her bus seat to a white passenger—triggering the 381-day bus boycott in Montgomery, Alabama, where the civil rights movement took a leap forward.

Mrs. Parks is still sought after to tell her unique story, a story nearly 44 years old. And rewards and honors have never stopped coming her way. Just this spring she was awarded the Congressional Gold Medal, the nation's highest civilian honor. And the University of Southern California plans to confer on her an honorary doctorate degree.

From New York to Washington, D.C. to California this nation is replete with Ladies in the Eighties, and it is refreshing to hear about them. A local look reveals a long list of such women right here in Kokomo.

Thelma Dougherty is "89 with a very sharp mind," says Volunteer Coordinator Rhonda Tiedemann. Thelma volunteers several days a week at St. Joseph Hospital. As a faithful worker, she has accumulated 6500 hours of volunteer service.

Thelma works at the Central Desk, where she serves as an information person assisting visitors to the hospital.

Marie Castor's 5,500 hours of volunteering at St. Joseph Hospital does not give a complete picture of how many hours she works to bring a smile or chuckle to the hospital patients who receive those Holiday Tray Favors.

Marie is the mastermind behind those clever creative holiday craft items that adorn the patient's trays at Halloween, Thanksgiving, Christmas, Valentine's Day and Easter.

These ladies and others in their age group are living proof that there is a refreshing alternative to being a "stagnant pond" person. Look around you! Ladies in the Eighties are everywhere, of every race and culture, from all walks of life.

1.7

Dorothy notes from personal experience that tragic events can bring communities together into a "family" that offers care. She tells the story of how residents in the apartment building where she lived were rescued from a fire. Men and women from the local fire department conducted rescue operations, and a nearby church provided shelter to those who were unexpectedly homeless.

Turtle Creek "family" came together during fire (*Kokomo Tribune*, July 10, 1997)

My claim to fame is that a firewall separated my apartment from the one that caught on fire July 10 at the Turtle Creek apartment complex.

After the fire was extinguished, miraculously, I found my apartment intact except for a thin layer of ash that settled on top of the in-house dust, and the pungent smell of smoke that had come in through the patio door. My patio and patio furniture, however, had heavy smoke damage.

After the residents' safe return to their apartments, there was time to grow calm and reflect on what had happened.

An elderly resident told me about her narrow escape. "My smoke alarm was going crazy! I knew the hall was full of smoke and I knew I move too slowly to make it down the hall without being overcome by smoke.

"So, I went out on my balcony." She remembers a big fireman climbing up a ladder, swinging onto her balcony, swooping her up and carrying her back through her apartment. Then moving fast down the hall and outside he called for someone to bring her a chair. Someone also gave her a blanket. "Everyone was so nice and kind," she said.

Another resident told me that she had just settled into a deep sound sleep when firemen broke down her door to wake her and get her out. She was so grateful for the rescue, she said, "For what they do they don't get paid enough."

Before the police, firetrucks, ambulances and Civil Defense arrived, Turtle Creek residents were banging on their neighbors' doors, rousing them from their beds and helping them exit the building. Susie Bell said she went banging on doors and "woke up older ladies I look out for."

"George and his wife, Betty, banged on my door and helped me get out," said Lena Magnuson. The hall was full of smoke, she remembers. One resident informed me that Apartment Manager Sharon Pope was also involved in alerting people to get out of bed and to leave the building, and she was one of the people Sharon had to wake up.

Rev. Walter J. Ungerer of the First Presbyterian Church got an early morning call asking him to open up the church as a temporary shelter. He, his custodian Jame Balger, and his business manager Fred Harris had restrooms, the Parlor, Fellowship Hall and coffee pot ready with amazing speed!

Susie Bell expressed the sentiments of the Turtle Creek residents when she said, "The firemen did a fantastic job of getting the fire under control. And I thank the church for opening their doors to us.

The professionally trained people, the volunteers, the Turtle Creek "family"—all working together made the best of a bad situation.

1.8

Throughout her life, Dorothy's social environment was urban. She grew up in Fort Wayne and lived in Evansville and Kokomo before moving back to Fort Wayne. However, she also demonstrated keen interest in rural community life, specifically the lifestyle of Amish and Mennonite people. Even though she did not use the term "Village" to describe their way of life, it is evident that she was intrigued by these communities and how they take care of each other.

> **Remembering Life during the Depression** (*Kokomo Tribune*, May 2, 1999)
>
> At some point in their lives, survivors of the Great Depression have undoubtedly asked themselves the "What if?" question: What if America is hit with another depression like the one in the 1930s? Clayton Sommers is one of those survivors who has pondered that question. And he is concerned about the young generation. "I don't know if they could survive." This octogenarian remembers 1930 to 1935 as the most difficult years of the Depression: "Those were tough times."
>
> Clayton grew up on a farm in rural Howard County during those tough times. Farm prices were extremely low. Grain sold for ten cents a bushel and hogs went for two and one half cents per pound. On one occasion when Clayton's father took a big load of hogs to market, his father made just enough money to pay his taxes and buy a pair of shoes.
>
> Many farmers who could not make enough money to pay their taxes lost their farms to the insurance companies that held the farmers' mortgages. Farmers who lost their farms would often work for other farmers who still had ownership of their farmlands.
>
> Foodwise, farm families were better off than townspeople because farms had livestock to butcher, cows for milk, chickens and eggs, and big gardens. Many town and city people had to depend on the bread lines for food.

Clayton says the Depression wasn't ALL bad because it brought out the best in most people. Hard times drew people closer. People cared about and helped each other. "Again and again when a neighbor got sick everybody went in, plowed his ground, and planted his fields." There were very few tractors in those days. Most farmers used workhorses. A few farmers preferred mules because they were tougher but ate less food.

Farm buggies were the common means of transportation for "goin' courtin'", for going to town or to faraway schools. Teachers drove buggies to school and kept them in "hack sheds." Clayton's brother had the special job of hitching up his teacher's buggy each school day at dismissal time.

The school Clayton attended from grades 1 to 12 still stands—-the Howard County School. He was a good student and won a scholarship to DePauw University at Greencastle, Indiana. The scholarship paid for tuition and books, but due to the Depression Clayton did not have the money to cover the other college expenses, so he could not attend DePauw.

Clayton married in 1935. He and his wife Ruth attended the Howard-Miami Mennonite Church. It was 2 miles from their farm. "Mennonites did not shy away from 'new things,'" says Clayton. When electricity became available and when indoor plumbing made its way to rural areas, Mennonites did not hesitate to use these modern conveniences. And when they had the money, Mennonites bought things like radios, telephones, tractors and cars. Clayton's father bought a car!!

Cars were not in general use. They were a rare sight. Some risk-taking car owners used kerosene in their car radiators because the price of alcohol was a couple dollars a gallon and kerosene cost about 15 cents a gallon. Yes, kerosene was much cheaper, but it was very dangerous to use. It also rotted out hoses more quickly.

The first radio Clayton remembers seeing was a Crystal Set with earphones. The radio reception was very poor. Telephones had two batteries in the phone box and when the batteries got weak, it was hard to hear voices over the telephone.

The Great Depression was just one of many significant events in Clayton's life. He and his wife Ruth raised three children—daughter Grace and sons Elson and Karl. Later on, Clayton entered the ministry, pastoring at Bon-Air Mennonite Church and then Parkview Mennonite Church. Today at age 86 and a widower, Clayton is still active at church helping as Sunday School teacher or song leader or wherever he is needed. He has "enjoyed a good life, the best."

As an octogenarian and as a survivor of the economic poverty of the Great Depression, Clayton has accumulated a wealth of captivating stories and priceless memories to pass on to his children and his children's children.

1.9

The vision for a mutually interdependent Village embracing people of diverse ethnic backgrounds and cultures has too often deteriorated into the opposite. After recalling the events of September 11, 2001, Dorothy wrote a column chronicling other historical acts of terrorism when people chose violent exclusion over loving embrace.

> **Terrorism was around way before 9–11** (*Kokomo Tribune*, January 6, 2004)
>
> According to TV news reports in late December, the U.S. Department of Homeland Security has decided to extend the "Orange Alert" indefinitely into the New Year. This "Orange Alert" that began during the Holiday Season rekindled memories of September 2001 with poignant comments and familiar graphic pictures.
>
> I think it is unnecessary to continually plead, "Remember 9–11." How could anyone forget? We remember that day in September!
>
> It would be worthwhile, however, to take another closer look at terrorism because the 21st century is not the only time in history when terrorism happened. Ancient unwritten oral history, then later on recorded

history told about "man's inhumanity to man" all around the world, everywhere.

My *World Book Encyclopedia* contains more terrorist information than I expected. "The word terrorism first appeared during the French Revolution (1789–1799)." Those 10 years were called the Reign of Terror.

In the 1930s, "Adolf Hitler of Germany, Benito Mussolini of Italy, and Joseph Stalin of the Soviet Union used terrorism to discourage opposition to their governments." Israel and Palestine terrorism began in 1948 and continues to this day. In the 1960s to 1980s, the Red Brigades in Italy committed terrorist acts. And in the 1990s, West Germany had the Red Army Faction to deal with.

After 9–11 many people were asking: What is a terrorist? How do we define "terrorism"? Most answers I heard and read were very brief and lacked details. So I was glad to read a more thorough definition in my *World Book Encyclopedia*. "Terrorism is the use or threat of violence to create fear and alarm. Terrorists murder and kidnap people, set off bombs, hijack airplanes, set fires and commit other serious crimes."

Terrorists also attack churches and synagogues, oil refineries and government offices. They choose any target certain to attract newspaper, internet and TV coverage. And terrorism crosses national boundaries.

A careful look at history reminds us that no continent is free from the taint of man's inhumanity to man. Each in its own way, at some point in history, has sunk to the low level of slavery, apartheid, the holocaust, the killing fields, genocide, ethnic cleansing or some other unspeakable evil. All are guilty—Europe, Asia, Africa, Australia, South America, North America. Maybe not Antarctica, I'm not sure; if only penguins could talk!

According to *World Book*: "Terrorist tactics have been used for hundreds of years. An American group, the Ku Klux Klan, used violence to terrorize blacks and their sympathizers in the periods following the end of the Civil War in 1865 and during the 1900s."

African American university professor and author, Cornel West labeled the systematic terrorism of lynching black men, black women and black children, "American

Terrorism." In America's dark past, more than 3445 African Americans were lynched, mostly in the South. But two black Hoosiers were lynched in 1930 in Marion, Indiana. And just five years ago, 1998, a black man, James Byrd, was lynched in Jasper, Texas.

Is a goal of peace replacing any and all forms of terrorism an untenable, pie-in-the-sky, cotton candy sentiment?

Years ago, Chester Crocker of the U.S. Institute of Peace suggested that our national interest would be well served if we vigorously pursued peace as a viable alternative, using better negotiation skills, more effective mediation, and a commanding influence in areas of conflict resolution.

Also some years ago, through Compromise Diplomacy, then Senator George Mitchell played a key role in bringing about peace in Northern Ireland where war had been raging for 25 years.

It should not go unnoticed that very recently Libya and the United States negotiated a peaceful agreement to get rid of weapons of mass destruction in that terrorist state.

Libya is said to be a "rogue nation" that harbors known terrorists. But "shock and awe" bombing did not bring about this surprising cooperation. Instead, it took nine months of "vigorously pursued peace," "better negotiation skills" and effective mediation, and a commanding influence of U.S. diplomatic persistence and patience to get the job done.

No, if the United States and Libya can come together at the negotiating table, surely the U.S. can bring other terrorist states "to the table." Of course, there will be naysayers. Never mind them. The impossible has already happened! This kind of success should be celebrated. It's time for an encore!

1.10

A topic that occasionally surfaces in Dorothy's columns is the festival of Kwanzaa, which takes place annually between Christmas and New Year's. Beginning in her early columns in the Evansville paper, *Our Times,* Dorothy highlights the family values emphasis in this movement. In her explanation of the principles of Kwanzaa it becomes apparent that, even though she doesn't use the term "Village," she sees this African holiday as a dynamic expression of the spirit of interdependence in the Village.

> **"Kwanzaa" defines family values** (*Kokomo Tribune,* December 21, 2000)
>
> Family values, family values, family values! People talk about them but what are they? About 35 years ago, Dr. M. "Ron" Karenga, a black studies professor in California, came up with an answer to that question. Karenga created and was founder of a family values holiday: "Kwanzaa."
>
> This seven-day holiday deliberately targets African-American families, and defines and demonstrates family values outlined in the Seven Principles of Kwanzaa. One principle is to be examined and practiced each day with the family or at a community gathering during Kwanzaa. Swahili is the language used to name the Seven Principles, a reminder to African-Americans of their African roots.
>
> The Seven Principles of Kwanzaa are: Unity, Self-determination, Collective work and responsibility, Cooperative Economics, Purpose, Creativity, and Faith.
>
> The Kwanzaa greeting card my sister Odessa sent me sums up the Kwanzaa holiday and Kwanzaa Principles in plain English. "Kwanzaa is a time to remember our history and to rekindle the flames of purpose, creativity and commitment to self and community. It is a time to surround ourselves with family and friends, to share the fruits of our labors. It is a time to celebrate our heritage, our faith, and our unity."
>
> Kwanzaa comes at just the right time—December 26 to January 1. Just in time as a respite from the

pre-Christmas commercial blitz, and a refreshing anti-
dote for the post-Christmas "blues." Kwanzaa in no way
replaces Christmas.

The Kwanzaa settings are often community-cen-
tered celebrations held in churches; sometimes in private
homes. In Evansville, Indiana, it is held at the Museum.
A few Decembers ago, IUK's Kelly House was the site
of a Kwanzaa gathering for the International Women of
Kokomo.

That snowless December evening, I was scheduled
to talk to these women about Kwanzaa. Also, at that time,
my son Bryce was thinking about getting a master's degree in mass communications. So I asked him to substi-
tute for me and be the speaker.

My challenge to Bryce was, "If you can explain
Kwanzaa to this international group from all over the
world, you are ready to tackle that master's degree." He
accepted the challenge. (I knew he would!)

Bryce emphasized in his Kwanzaa presentation
how much we all had in common,—purpose, creativity,
faith. And he appreciated the supportive comment made
by Afsaneh (from Iran): The Persian word for "Faith" is
very similar to the Swahili word imani (Faith).

The first time Maria (from the Philippines) heard
about Kwanzaa was at Bryce's "lecture." Consequently,
at her second Kwanzaa event, Maria was already well
informed about that holiday. The second Kwanzaa experience took place in the Kokomo home of Naima (from
Ghana) and her family.

Maria, husband Patrick and daughters Kim and
Alex felt the full welcome of an inclusive, warm family
atmosphere. They were guests and Kwanzaa participants
too. For daughters Kim and Alex, this exposure was better than a talk at school, or just reading a book about
Kwanzaa. "They lived it!"

If you can't "live it" then Linda Robertson's book,
The Complete Kwanzaa Celebration Book, is one of the
resources available to anyone wanting a broader understanding of this Afrocentric family values holiday.

I PONDER. . .

Having read these columns I imagine myself engaged in conversation with Dorothy in a diverse group (ethnically, politically, social status). We talk about the nature and scope of our Village. A tool we might use to get the conversation going could be this check list (check all that apply). Is my Village

- A collection of members of my social group of likeminded individuals who support each other?
- An ethnically diverse multi-cultural network of encouragement, challenge and critique?
- A network of public services providing protection and care during emergencies?
- A supremacist group ready to force compliance to our views?
- The global community in which resources are generously shared?
- Other?

2

Family

DOROTHY PICTURES THE VILLAGE as an interconnected community that embraces individuals and families. The Village furnishes the fabric within which families find their identity. The Village is like a family, an interconnected web of relationships between parents and their children, between men and women, and among people of all ages. From the perspective of families beset by tensions and brokenness it becomes apparent that families sometimes need a boost from the Village to restore healthy relationships.

There are frequent references to Dorothy's friends and acquaintances in her newspaper columns but members of her family are rarely mentioned. Alert readers of the articles transcribed in this collection will notice a few references to them.

Some of Dorothy's personal letters to friends were forwarded to me when I was gathering information about her early life. In her files was a rather extensive contact list of people with whom she had corresponded with some regularity. That list became my source of names and addresses for my annual Christmas letters to inform her friends and several nieces and nephews about how

Dorothy was doing. Many of the recipients of these letters responded by sharing about their relationship with Dorothy.

Dorothy's nephew Gordon Paschall replied to my letters on
several occasions. A letter dated September 26, 2015 opens a window into Dorothy's family life:

> Mr. Elias. I would like to thank you for forwarding my
> aunt Dorothy's mail. I hadn't heard from her in quite
> some time. And when she did last write I could detect
> from her handwriting that something was up. So it's
> increased dementia? I am so sorry to hear about that. I
> work around a lot of seniors so I have some idea of what
> it is like.
>
> Just for your information. I lived with aunt Dorothy
> towards the end of my teenage years. Of course, she was
> married at the time. And my mother (Dorothy's sister)
> was deemed unfit to care for me at that time. I gradu-
> ated from high school and moved out of her home. (I was
> actually put out by her husband Calvin.) Anyway we lost
> contact with each other, until my mother died, and I sent
> aunt Dorothy an obituary. Then we were back in touch
> again. I've yet to hear from her son Bryce Daniel. When I
> am in a position to travel up there to Goshen I will do so.

Among letters I received from friends was one from Sandy
Todd, whose experience mirrors that of many others:

> (Dorothy) and I have been what might be most accurate-
> ly called pen pals. We met at Indiana University in the
> summer of 1955 (before our senior year in high school)
> at Girls State. We have corresponded ever since then. I
> usually send her a Christmas card and brief letter and she
> usually sends me a letter in January.

For the most part, Dorothy's files do not include copies of
letters that she had written. However, Grace Sommers Whitehead, her college roommate and lifelong friend, kept letters that
Dorothy had sent to her. Grace wanted to unclutter her files so
she passed these letters on to me. Two quotations from these letters may be appropriate here to provide glimpses into Dorothy's
personal life. Both illustrate her self-deprecating humor. One is an

acknowledgment of a birthday card (dated February 13, 1965) on the occasion of Dorothy's 27th birthday:

> Thanks for the birthday card—the big day was yesterday! Lincoln and I share this event. We have some other things in common too. Both of us are both honest and homely.

In the other citation she updates Grace about her marriage and her experience when she was pregnant with their child. With tongue firmly in her cheek she gave this child the name Calva Ree, likely intended as a gender neutral version of her husband Calvin's name expanded into a somewhat dubious allusion to the hill where Jesus died:

> Well, I know my courtship was never as interesting as yours! Of course, yours is a little longer than ours was. But you have more "items of concern" than we did, it seems to me.
>
> My two hang-ups were 1) I don't like preachers; and 2) I didn't think blind people could be very independent. As usual I was wrong on both counts. I saw what the blind can do, if they have the will, brain power, etc. And as for preachers . . . I learned to be tolerant of them (especially him).
>
> Went to my doctor last Monday. Calva Ree is breached again. Calva constantly rotates. "It" should be in one position—head down. But it rotates, revolves, and prefers a "standing position" with head under my ribs and feet kicking me in the intestines. Therefore I am again a candidate for surgery. After an X-ray on June 2nd the doctor will know more what to do with the "orbiting offspring." (Letter dated May 21, 1970)

Dorothy's newspaper articles dealt with a number of family themes but not with the same level of personal candor evident in her letters. Some of her friends describe their relationship with the kind of intimacy one might expect within a family. Before we hear from Dorothy about the roles of mothers and fathers in nurturing children we'll tune in to some reflections by her friend, Mary Kraft:

I considered (Dorothy) a true and faithful friend. I am not sure where to start when describing my relationship with her. First of all, she was the kind of friend that I could call on when I had no one else to turn to. She had a unique way of sharing lessons with me. She would say, "Remember Lot's wife! Don't look back." That was her way of telling me that once I had made the right decision regarding someone or something not to waver, lament, or regret. She also taught me that when you are doing a business transaction with a friend always to keep good records and receipts because you could lose a dear friend over one incident. One of the most important things she taught me was to take care of solemn decisions such as funeral pre-arrangements on a bright and sunny day.

There is so much more I could say, like when she would babysit my boys. She always played classical music when they napped. She was never the typical friend, just watching the kids a couple of hours. They would do arts and crafts and more. Then take that classical music nap. I always wanted to nap too when I came to pick them up. I miss "Word" as I called her. I miss her jokes, the laughs we shared. She will always be with me in spirit.

DOROTHY'S WORD

2.1

Many of Dorothy's columns are written in ways that clearly reveal her professional identity as a teacher. References to her family life and her experience as a parent occur less often. However, looking back as a teacher she realizes afresh the formative role of the family in child development.

She thinks about the art of quality listening. Does the child feel heard?

Hey, anybody listening? (Kokomo Tribune, August 1, 1998)
Joyce strummed her guitar and sang:

"Hey, hey! Anybody listening? Hey, hey! Anybody care?"

That song always reminded me of my biggest regret in teaching—not having enough quality listening time. Not enough time to really give an attentive ear to the many children who needed to be heard, who had something to say that really mattered to them.

All through my teaching years there was a time restraint—pledging allegiance to the time clock, to tight schedules and deadlines. Nevertheless, I decided to include "Show & Tell" in my classroom schedule as a deliberate attempt at quality listening. My students understood that this set-aside time was not about competition or comparisons; not about who had the latest toy or who was wearing the newest designer outfit. Rather it was primetime for each child to have the undivided attention of the class, to be the central focus as he/she determined what "really important stuff" to share with the group.

Important stuff like: Alice's skinned arm, William's live butterfly, Abby's piece of petrified wood, Cynthia's sea shells, Sheryl's tobacco leaf, Joey's missing tooth and his green bug, Pamela's snake skin, Daniel's cocoon, fossil and maracas, Peggy's dead bees in a jar. Sometimes parents were pulled into the act—bringing in caged pets or even a new baby brother or sister as part of someone's "Show and Tell" time.

Chinese scholar, journalist, author Lin Yu Tang wrote: "Besides the noble art of getting things done is the noble art of leaving things undone." I'm glad I left a few things undone, at least temporarily, to listen one-on-one. Patricia wanted to explain her reason for being tardy again. The alarm clock didn't go off, she said, so the whole family "over-woke." Roy Eric need to confront me—"Why can't we get drinks when we want to, like the 2nd and 3rd Grades?"

Kim wanted a private moment to tell me about her amazing discovery. "I saw a praying mantis, and it prayed!" And Randy just wanted to be clear: "I don't like school." Patricia, Roy, Eric, Kim, Randy and countless other children are not necessarily wanting feedback, advice, answers; sometimes they just want to be heard. And the most appropriate response is to listen.

One mother told me that she is the envy of her friends because she and her teenage daughter talk regularly about school or any other topic that needs to be discussed. I am convinced that this happy mother laid the foundation for these "sharing times" with quality listening she practiced back in her daughter's early years. I like to think I practice quality listening when my teacher friend, Janice, phones me and invariably says: "Knock on wood! Thank your lucky stars! Be glad you're out!" She means out-of-teaching, retired. I remind Janice that I'm not completely out of teaching: "I'm tutoring. It's the ideal situation. Interested students, supportive parents."

My classroom teaching was geared primarily to fast-track group learning, but tutoring allows the luxury of slowed down, full-time, one-on-one teaching. I see tutoring as quality teaching PLUS quality listening time. Listening to what the student needs to express or wants to share. Youngsters I know about come from fast-track homes where there is not enough SLOW in the family schedule. Too often their need to be heard goes unfulfilled. The fast-track world can and should stop at the tutoring door.

Effective tutoring provides a learning/listening environment where the students' sense of importance enhances their self-esteem. If first they believe (in themselves) then they will achieve. One of my supportive parents is a grandmother who says her grandson, Tyrece and his teacher are very pleased with the progress Tyrece has made with tutoring assistance. Johnathan likes how he and mom work on his tutoring homework together. And Lin pats himself on the back because he is "so much smarter now" and is looking forward to third grade.

First they believe, then they achieve. Hey, hey! Anybody listening?

2.2

In her long career as a teacher Dorothy undoubtedly dealt with children whose conduct on the playground and elsewhere demonstrated the lack of healthy conflict resolution skills. Often their behavior reflects family patterns, she suggests. Even though there may not be a direct cause and effect relationship, lack of listening sometimes leads to bullying. Bullies arrive at school ready-made from a place called home, and the school becomes the setting where such behavior often plays itself out.

Book suggest ways to deal with a bully (*Kokomo Tribune,* August 15, 2000)

I retired five years ago but I still remember those dreaded ISTEP tests. If my second hand information is correct, the ISTEP tests for third graders include writing an essay on a given topic. I have an essay question but it certainly won't appear on the ISTEP test: When is a goat not a goat? (When it's a scapegoat.)

A scapegoat is a person who bears the blame of others, a person who has to shoulder the blame of others, a person who has to shoulder all the blame. In other words, a scapegoat is the person who gets picked on. And for students who are picked on, "Back to School" are three words that are as unwelcome as dandelions in a well-manicured lawn.

My friend's oldest son, Matthew, attends the junior high school in Newburgh, a suburb of Evansville. Matthew is black, athletic, and makes good grades. His ISTEP scores are high. About a year ago, for whatever reason, Matthew was the scapegoat of some school bullies.

Matthew's birthday was in July and I almost sent him a Benjamin Franklin Award book for his birthday. Instead, I sent him a card and birthday money. I kept the book and read it myself.

Why is Everybody Always Picking on Me? A Guide to Understanding Bullies for Young People by Terrence Webster-Doyle is the book I almost mailed to Matthew. It is a book that cannot compete with the "Harry Potter" craze. It is a "how-to" book based on the real world. A book that suggests ways to solve conflicts nonviolently in our violent society.

Webster-Doyle dedicated this book to "young people who have been bullied and who want to understand this problem and deal with it creatively." The book is also dedicated to young people who bully others so they can learn "healthy, peaceful ways to get what they want."

This author was bullied a lot as he was growing up. "I am now fifty years old and I still remember how it felt. . . That's why I've written this book."

Bullies come in all sizes, ages and nationalities, he wrote. They can be rich or poor, educated or ignorant, male or female. This is what bullies have in common: They verbally or physically pick on others, and they are people who are hurt, angry, afraid and frustrated.

Why is Everybody Always Picking on Me? is a guidebook with a workbook format. There is a list that defines 11 types of bullies. There are short stories that illustrate important points, roleplaying skits, questions with space for responses and opportunities for journaling.

I think Matthew would have been motivated to share some of these ideas with his younger brother, Jonathan, who will attend the junior high in a few years.

Contrary to popular belief, schools do not make bullies, and kids are not born bullies. Nevertheless, bullies seem to arrive at school "ready-made" from a place called home. Unfortunately, school is a place where bullying is acted out in front of a captive audience, and where there is an ample supply of scapegoats.

Back-to-School is a good time for parents, teachers and other caring adults to unite and work toward zero tolerance of bullying. Webster-Doyle said, "If we can begin to create programs directed at understanding this issue of bullying, then we will help raise a generation of young people who will have the possibility of being free from its devastating effects."

This school year is just getting underway and that's when school bullies also start up. Webster-Doyle's book is definitely a Back-to-School survival book, so I think I'll send it to Matthew after all.

2.3

Rituals in family life have a significant role in shaping identity and character for children. Dorothy found herself thinking about birthdays and how they are celebrated.

Famous Birthday Song was actually written by two Educators (*Kokomo Tribune*, September 25, 1999)

It is sung almost everywhere! It is sung in homes and schools, in concert halls and night clubs, in churches and in the White House. Once I heard it sung in the Indiana General Assembly—apparently preceded by unanimous consent.

I am proud to know that this song was written by two educators—one a kindergarten teacher, the other a principal—Mildred and her sister, Dr. Patty Hill. The year was 1893, the place—Louisville, Ky.

This song is an equal opportunity song. It belongs to everybody, but a court ruled, "Every time the song is sung for commercial purposes, they (the Hill sisters) are entitled to a royalty." This song is The Birthday Song, better known as "Happy Birthday to You."

Originally this song was called "Good Morning to All." Years later, Robert H. Coleman changed the second verse to "Happy Birthday to You." Coleman published the song and included his new second verse without getting proper permission. The court ruled against Coleman even though "Happy Birthday to You" became so popular that the first verse was dropped.

In some areas of the world there are people who are nameless, never given a name. Some child advocacy groups are urging that children everywhere receive the personal identity a name provides.

Evidently, a person can live a lifetime without a name, but no one can live without a birthday. That birthday may or may not be acknowledged or celebrated—but it is, nevertheless, "the day on which one is born." A birthday card for my son, Bryce, put it this way: "We all have 'em—Birthdays."

When I asked 89-year-old Janice Walker about her birthday memories, she told me birthday celebrations

were not a big event in her family when she was growing up. In her home a birthday party was family-focused
and simple: a cake, no ice cream. Quite different from
birthday parties nowadays.

Janice (pronounced "Jan-niece") and her twin sister, Berniece "got a few gifts and that's about it" on their
birthdays. "In those days you couldn't afford much, especially where there were two."

Janice said their friends were not excluded from
the birthday celebrations. "We had fun—good clean
fun, playing games, running, laughing and talking with
school friends. You had to make your own fun."

Janice and Berniece dressed alike until their 13th
birthday, then "we broke that up." A few years later, the
twins went their separate ways. Berniece married and
moved 100 miles away. Janice married but stayed in
Kokomo.

Janice remembers a special birthday celebration
that happened almost 10 years ago. A cousin took Janice
(and her husband) and Berniece out to dinner in Elkhart
for their 80th birthday, probably their fanciest birthday
celebration. In the year 2000, the twins will be 90 and
entitled to ANY kind of party they want!

Ways of celebrating birthdays have changed a lot
down through the years, yet some celebrants have maintained the family-focused emphasis that Janice and Berniece experienced when they were growing up.

Debbie Midcalf of California hangs a string of balloons over the dining room table a week before her child's
birthday. "All the balloons are the same color, except for
the birthday balloon. Every day we pop one balloon and
count down one more day" until finally it is the birthday!

Julie Stockler of Pennsylvania gets up in the middle
of the night and goes into the birthday child's room and
decorates with balloons, sparklers, crepe paper, "all that
stuff." Then the "birthday fair" leaves a trail of glitter
that goes out the bedroom door, through the house, and
down the driveway.

Birthdays—we all have 'em. Happy Birthday to you!

2.4

The themes that Dorothy addresses in her columns were generally not chosen in line with the calendar. There are exceptions, such as Martin Luther King Day (January), Thanksgiving (November), and Christmas (December). In addition, in May and June Dorothy typically focuses on family themes, specifically Mother's Day and Father's Day. The articles included below are representative of the ones that she submitted annually on these special family occasions.

The Miracle of Parenting (*Kokomo Tribune*, June 16, 2003)

Overkill is any effect or result that far exceeds what is necessary. For example, an elementary student's assignment was to make a report on penguins. This was before the hi-tech era, back in the days when a library was a library, not a Media Center with a computer lab.

The librarian (not a media specialist) brought the student books and magazines on the subject. Then more books, more magazines and some encyclopedias. Finally the student spoke up. "I don't what to know that much about penguins." Overkill.

On today's information super highway there is abundant "fatherhood" research data, much "fatherly" advice, easy access to information on parenting by fathers. Sincere, devoted fathers could be intimidated by so many sources and resources. Overkill?

Researchers at Pennsylvania State University and the University of California's Riverside Center for Family Studies say the father's role in parenting is important, and the father-child bond is a unique bond. (I think fathers already know that.)

Some researches view fatherhood as a complex job "with huge consequences for the emotional and intellectual growth of children." Also, they point out that fathers' parenting is different from mothers'. (Who doesn't know that?)

The experts at Santa Clara University advise fathers to "be involved from the beginning." Mr. Earl Woods, father of Tiger Woods, did that. Mr. Richard Williams, father of Venus and Serena Williams, did that. They got involved and stayed involved, and their children, the sports world in particular and the public in general are all beneficiaries of that fatherly involvement.

Sports Illustrated writer Rick Reilly is quoted in the 1998 "Father and Son" edition: "From the time he was a preschool prodigy, Tiger Woods has prospered according to his father's plan."

Earl Woods wisely observed that "black kids grew up with basketball or football or baseball from the time they could walk. The game became part of them from the beginning. But they learned golf too late. Not Tiger. Tiger knew how to swing a golf club before he could walk.

The Woods, father and son, had this motto: "Expect the best, prepare for the worst." And the father's message to parents was: "If you treat your child with admiration, respect and love, a miracle will occur."

Tiger Woods is certainly "a gold miracle." Look at his amazing record. Look at his age. He says, "My father was a Green Beret. He had to endure a lot. He passed his toughness on to me."

Mr. Williams certainly was "involved from the beginning." It was he who started daughters Venus and Serena on their way to become world-class tennis layers. He was their tennis coach at their home in inner-city Compton, California, when both girls were very young.

Serena wrote a tennis tale about older sister Venus, something that happened a long time ago but reveals the kind of determination her sister had from the beginning. "A 4-year-old girl in Compton, California began to cry. She wasn't crying because she lost her doll or because she was hurt. She was crying because her dad wouldn't let her hit all the tennis balls in the grocery cart."

Nowadays both of these young champions are at the top of their game—singles titles, double crowns, U.S. Open, Wimbledon, the Olympics, and the rest is history—with their protective father ever nearby.

One day *Ebony Magazine* writer Kevin Chappell went grocery shopping and took his 2-year-old daughter with him. He said all eyes were fixed on him, wondering what he was up to. (Not much has changed for the black male.)

How sad to be the center of attention simply because a black male is being a responsible father. Why should it be shocking to see a young black father continuing "the tradition set by our fathers and their fathers"?

Chappell says he doesn't want to be praised and patted on the back for doing "something as fundamentally right as caring for the child I helped bring into the world." He added, "I want to be ignored, let alone—nobody extraordinary, just a black father."

Well, on June 6, an early afternoon at Aldi's I saw a young black father. Yes, I too stared at him. But I also wanted to pat him on the back. I wanted to praise him for grocery shopping with three young daughters. There was no running, yelling or whining. How refreshing!

As Tiger's dad said, "If you treat your child with admiration, respect and love, a miracle will occur." And grocery shopping will be a lot more pleasant!

2.5

Another of Dorothy's family-related articles highlights exemplary fathers whose devotion helped their children to excel. She even salutes several dads who faithfully take their children to her tutoring sessions.

Cheers to 'faithful fathers' (*Kokomo Tribune*, June 2000)
Some of us vividly remember superstar pop singer Diana Ross and her many hit songs, including "Reach out and touch somebody's hand, make this a better world if you can." But reaching out and touching and making this a better world antedates Diana Ross and her popular song.

The Black Church from its very beginning was committed to reaching out, to making a better world. From the very beginning, black church leadership and influential father figures went about touching lives. Dr. Charles Tindley is a renowned example.

Tindley (1856–1933) was a minister for 30 years in Philadelphia, Pennsylvania, and a prolific hymn writer. One of the many people he reached out to and touched was Thomas A. Dorsey. Dorsey was forever grateful for that father-figure influence on his life.

Tindley persuaded and inspired Dorsey to leave the vaudeville and blues circuits and redirect his musical talents to writing religious music exclusively. Dorsey began writing gospel songs in the 1920s and produced more than 400 songs. In 1932 Dorsey composed his most popular gospel song which still enjoys universal appeal: "Precious Lord, Take my Hand."

Preacher/leader Wallace McLaughlin at the Fathers Resource Center in Indianapolis reaches out to touch the lives of young African-American fathers, and tries to make this a better world for them and their families.

"The work that I do, I dedicate to the memory of my father (a minister) who died when I was 13," said McLaughlin. "He gave me a sense of life and an understanding of fatherhood and what I am called to do."

The Fathers Resource Center's mission is to improve the life-chances of children by helping young fathers achieve self-sufficiency and strengthen their parental involvement.

Some of the activities going on at the Center are: an intense 6-week Fatherhood Development Workshop, parental and co-parental classes, employment counseling, job placement and retention services, and long-term career planning. Also, fathers are prepared to sign a child support agreement.

"A man's identity is locked up in what he does and what he produces, not what he is as husband and father," said Ken Canfield, founder and president of the National Center for Fathering in Kansas. The challenge for working fathers is to find a balance between being a breadwinner and a family man. There are few role models.

Books like *Working Fathers* and *Business Dad: How Good Businessmen Can Make Great Fathers (and Vice Versa)* offer some guidance for the balancing act of work versus wife and kids.

Deadbeat dads and absentee fathers are found in all ethnic groups and races, on all economic levels. The good news is that there are fathers from all ethnic groups and races, on all economic levels, who do "have a life" with their families and are trying to make this a better world, especially for their children.

I have observed four faithful fathers who spend time transporting their kids to and from after-school tutoring classes. These dads deserve report cards full of good grades for making good attendance possible, for modeling good manners and respect, and for showing genuine caring and concern for their children's best interests.

Three cheers for these dads: Mr. Ewbank (Albert's dad), Mr. Barrett (Johnathan's dad), Mr. Castillo (Anzaya's dad), and Mr. Clark (Asha's and Shawn's dad).

2.6

In articles during May Dorothy predictably turns to Mother's Day themes. She notes that for some people this day always evokes sad memories. Her own mother had died during her freshman year in college. Another scenario for some people is that they become primary caregivers for their mothers in their old age. When I read the anecdote that Dorothy shares about a young woman who regularly mothers her mother in a care home I remember that when we arrived for our regular visits Lillian always hugged and kissed Dorothy. We like to think that this embrace helped Dorothy to remember her mother. When COVID restrictions made such visits (and the accompanying opening embrace) impossible, she (and we) missed these moments of intimate remembering.

Sunday 'special' day' (*Kokomo Tribune*, May 13, 2000)
In Yugoslavia it is two Sundays before Christmas. In England it is called Mothering Sunday and comes about three months before Easter. But in the U.S.A. Mother's Day is the second Sunday in May.

The dates differ and the ways of celebrating may vary but Mother's Day around the world is a special time set aside to honor mothers. Some mothers will be honored in the old traditional ways. Others will be treated to new and unique experiences.

On the same day, however, some mothers will not be celebrated but mourning—mothers who have lost children by death or drugs or other tragedies. And some motherless children on Mother's Day will feel their loss and perhaps identify with the words of the old Negro Spiritual: "Sometimes I feel like a motherless child, Sometimes I feel like a motherless child, A long ways from home, A long ways from home."

A week before Christmas (December 1999) one of my nieces died unexpectedly. A few days after the funeral her son mentioned how difficult it was going to be coping with holidays like Mother's Day. I understood his feelings because my mother died when I was a freshman in college, "a long ways from home" and Mother's Day became, for me, a dreaded holiday for a very long time.

Often a lasting tribute honoring a mother's memory can help ease the loss. That's one way Cynthia Cooper handled her loss. Her story is told in *Clarity Magazine*.

"My mother was a remarkable lady," said Cynthia. "I saw her struggle and persevere through a lot of tough times for us (8) kids. I learned my work ethic from her."

When her mother died of cancer, Cynthia developed a nonprofit foundation that donates money to cancer organizations, and another foundation that benefits inner-city children who have cancer.

Cynthia Cooper is "the Michael Jordan of woman's basketball" and the top scorer for the Houston Comets. Last September she led her team to its third consecutive WNBA Championship. Cynthia's mother was her inspiration. She enjoyed watching Cynthia play basketball and never missed a game until she became too ill to attend.

For a growing population of adult children Mother's Day is forever altered because they are trapped in a role reversal that requires them to "mother" their mothers as old age takes over. In the May issue of *Daily Word*,

Colleen Zuck looks at the past, and also at how different things are today as she "mothers" her mother.

"I let memories of my mother fill my mind. Throughout my growing-up years, her kiss had eased both my emotional and physical hurts. She had always been there for me whenever I needed her, doing everything she could think of to make me feel better.

"Momma is in a special-care unit now, near my work and home so I can visit her every day. I love to hug and kiss her—my attempt to keep her from slipping farther away from me."

"Mother's Day will be a day of aching emptiness for the young woman I met last month who told me her mother was brutally murdered. This distraught daughter said her mother had been "a good mother" and didn't deserve to die that way. What a horrendously traumatic burden this grieving daughter is bearing."

To find solace and begin healing is a SLOW process, but I hope this young woman will someday be able to turn her raw pain and deep suffering into celebrating good memories of her mother.

2.7

Rituals around Mother's Day often exclude some people. Dorothy celebrates an event that allowed her to bring her son to what was normally billed as a "mother and daughter" occasion. She found joy in participating in a "mother and child" event. She also feels strongly that women who "mother love" children need to be recognized, whether or not they have ever given birth.

Include all mothers in Sunday's celebration (*Kokomo Tribune*, May 8, 1999)

Last year in May, those seven sacred words "we have never done it that way" did not stop a new venture for Faith United Methodist Church, Kokomo. The new venture was their first Mother-Child Brunch! The mother-daughter traditionalists, deeply rooted in the status quo, may have found the change unsettling, but it was an inclusive occasion for people like me. . .daughterless. I appreciated being able to have my son Bryce with me at that mother celebration.

If the Mother-Child Brunch becomes a widespread event, that will be a step in the right direction. Daughterless mothers would no longer be excluded from the many pre-Mother's Day festivities. But we must go one step farther and make sure all mothers are included on Mother's Day as well: birth mothers, adoptive mothers, single mothers, stepmothers, foster mothers, grandmothers, foster grandmothers.

I disagree with the notion that Mother's Day should only honor those females who go through the birthing process. Remember, some females who go through the birthing process leave their newborns in restrooms, dumpsters, on doorsteps, or take them home to be unloved. The true spirit of Mother's Day celebrates all women who mother-love children from babyhood to adulthood whether they are the biological mothers or someone else.

Mother's Day ranks second only to Christmas in the number of phone calls made in a single day; and only Thanksgiving Day brings more people to restaurants in the United States than does Mother's Day, according to the National Restaurant Association.

Freelance writer Pamela Kennedy suggested that mothers have an extra sense called "Mothersense." It is as ancient as humanity, yet always informed and up-to-date, and can tell in an instant if you're "going nowhere fast" or "heading for trouble."

Mothersense, sometimes renamed Mother's Wisdom, was what the late Marian Anderson was referring to when she said: "My mother taught me you can't do anything by yourself. There's always somebody to make the stone flat for you to stand on." Putting her mother's words into action, contralto Marian Anderson made "the stone flat" by permanently breaking down the color barrier at the Metropolitan Opera in 1955, and later establishing Marian Anderson Scholarships for African-Americans wanting to pursue singing careers in opera.

Shirley Verrett, Grace Brumbry, Jesse Norman, Leontyne Price, Denyce Graves and Kathleen Battle are marvelously talented opera divas ever aware that Marian Anderson made "the stone flat" for them to stand/sing on.

My friend Sybil lives in the Republic of Panama. She calls her American-born grandchildren "my grands." She bemoans the fact that she lives too far away to "make the stones flat" for them. Her newest "grand," a granddaughter, was born in Kentucky a little more than a year ago. Sybil is a retired nurse who worked in a maternity ward her last eight years at the U.S. military hospital in Panama. She liked the "Baby Ward" the best. "That was my favorite place to work," she said.

Mothersense is bestowed on all mothers of all races and walks of life, the famous and the unsung. Josephine Riley Matthews or "Mama Jo" is a shining example. She was a licensed mid-wife for 40 years in Aiken County, S.C. She safely delivered more than 1300 babies, black and white, in rural South Carolina. And she said, "I'll bet you one thing. If the man had to have the first baby there wouldn't be but two in the family. Yes sir, let him have the first one and the woman the second one, and his time wouldn't come around no more."

I PONDER. . .

Having read these columns I imagine myself engaged in conversation with Dorothy about how our families of origin shaped us.

- Did we feel heard?
- Were we being nurtured to be gentle and kind toward friends, and accepting toward people who were different from us?

I might talk about our experience when Lillian and I were renting an apartment from an African American couple, Simon and Bessie. After we had moved to an apartment that provided space to accommodate our second child, we periodically came back for visits. Our daughter, age 18 months, was delighted to sit again on Simon's lap. After a few moments together she looked up at him and said, "You're black!" His immediate response to her was, "Laurel Dawn, hadn't you noticed that before?" We realized then that for our child, living in this African American home had felt comfortable and normal. It was only after we had moved into an apartment where everyone was white that she began to notice the difference.

- I might ask Dorothy, "Could you share about your experience as a child, and later as an adult, living among and working with predominantly white people?"

- Surely she would invite me to talk about growing up in a rural German speaking Mennonite family with minimal contact with people who were "other."

- What are we learning about parenting?

Another dynamic that Dorothy mentions has to do with Mother's Day and Father's Day activities that exclude people who although they have not birthed children have active mothering and fathering impact on children. She also notes that public perceptions of men sometimes imply that they do not nurture their children.

- What have you experienced?

- What have you observed?

3

School

WHEN I CONSIDERED HOW to arrange this collection of short newspaper articles I found myself coming time and again to the rubric of Dorothy as teacher. A bulletin that Lillian and I prepared for the graveside service quotes Isaiah 50:4a: "The Lord has given me the tongue of a teacher, that I may know how to sustain the weary with a word." Dorothy had included this text in a journal that she had apparently started when she stopped writing newspaper columns. It seemed to us that it served as a succinct summary of her identity and vocation. As the articles gathered in this collection demonstrate, she had also discovered the pen as a tool to inform, encourage, chide and instruct.

Dorothy's writings clearly convey her awareness that she had been taught. Likely she had not noticed that the NRSV translation of Isaiah 50:4a has a marginal note indicating that the original might have read, "The Lord has given me the tongue of those who are taught." The last half of Isaiah 50:4 corroborates this understanding: "Morning by morning (God) wakens my ear to listen as those who are taught."

Sorting through a file of her clippings I discovered that Dorothy had saved an article written about her for a local Fort Wayne paper. It was published in 1954 when she was a junior in High School! She reflected on how she was taught and how she learned:

Honor Student Studies Difficult Homework First

"Good study habits are definitely the most important factor in getting good grades." This statement was recently made by Dorothy Phinezy, a junior. Dorothy, who has always been a good student, has the ardent belief that her fine grades are the consequences of hard, well organized study.

One of Dorothy's main ideas of study is to do as much as possible at school, throughout the day. "I usually have at least half of my homework done at 3:20," says Dorothy. When she does her work at home, Dorothy does her most difficult subjects first, while her mind is still refreshed, and not confused.

As far as hard subjects are concerned, Dorothy says she has the hardest time with math, while art seems to come easily. However, English is her favorite subject. Dorothy's ambitions include the vocations of either nursing or elementary teaching.

As in every other system, problems do arise, and so it is with studying. "There are times when things come up that might throw a monkey wrench into your schedule, if you don't have strong will power," recalled Dorothy. "With football games, shows, parties, and the other activities, temptations of not studying mount and mount," continued Dorothy.

"A big influence on your study habits is made by your teachers," Dorothy explained. "There are some teachers who make you feel as if you want to study, while others discourage you." She also definitely believes that studying now will pay off in big dividends in the future. If you develop a good study system now you will find it is easier to organize other such systems, such as a budget.

Dorothy leaves one suggestion with the freshmen: "Start studying now, don't wait until your last year to make good grades. Remember, you make your grades, your teachers don't."

This clipping from a Fort Wayne newspaper suggests that one of her teachers may have alerted a staff writer to a potential story about a promising student. This was an article written not by Dorothy but about her. And it conveys early hints that this gifted teenager would someday become a teacher.

DOROTHY'S WORD

Readers of Dorothy's newspaper columns are frequently reminded that indeed she did become a teacher and that she did most of her writing as a retiree looking back on a long teaching career. This teacher's pen reminds us that families are embraced by the interconnected network, the Village, an extended family, an embracing community. A key expression of this supportive community is the school. Dorothy frequently recalls her own experience as a child in Fort Wayne schools. She rehearses memories from her years as a college student, especially at Goshen College and Marion College. Many of her articles feature her rich experiences as an elementary school teacher: the classroom, the children, her style as teacher, her relationship with her colleagues, her interaction with parents.

What always inspired me to visualize Dorothy's students was a framed display of handprints that was hanging above her bed in the care homes where she lived her last years. These handprints were created by the last class that Dorothy taught before her retirement in 1995. They speak with silent eloquence about their teacher's imprint on their lives. I wonder how many of these children, now adults, might be stimulated by these writings to remember their teacher, Ms. Word.

Dorothy clearly thrived as a teacher. However, she did not sugarcoat the difficulties that she faced as a black woman facing discrimination on the basis of race and often working in classrooms that were inadequately equipped. The lingering legacy of segregation made itself known in ongoing inequality.

3.1

Several of Dorothy's columns narrate her encounters with racism in the school systems. She also provides some of the historical background, including the landmark Supreme Court 1954 ruling in the Brown vs. School Board case. This historic event was often her topic of choice for columns that she wrote in in the month of May. In 1997 she takes a historical perspective. What happened to the Brown family whose case was presented to the court for resolution?

> **Segregated schools often received the 'throwaways"**
> (*Kokomo Tribune*, May 28, 1997)
> Forty-three years ago, in the month of May, the U.S. Supreme Court declared an end to legal school segregation. There were to be no "separate but equal" public schools. That landmark decision was known as Brown versus the School Board of Education of Topeka, Kansas. Oliver Brown was representing his daughter, Linda, and several other African-American minors. I don't know how old Linda was on that historic day. I saw her picture in the newspapers and magazines. She was dressed in her Sunday best, ruffles and ribbons! She looked like a very young elementary student surrounded by her father, Oliver Brown, and victorious lawyers. Thurgood Marshall was the chief counsel and anchorman of the legal team for the Browns. Marshall later returned to the Supreme Court as the first African American to serve as a Supreme Court judge.
> I often wondered what happened to Linda Brown after that desegregationist ruling. I was scared for her, worried that she might become the target of some violent act. It was a scary and dangerous time to be an African American. Nightriders were still terrorizing black people. Lynchings, shootings and bombings were still happening. School integration and court-ordered busing only broadened the anger and outrage.
> For a long time, I was under the illusion that if Linda Brown "came north" she would be safe. Then I encountered prejudice and racism northern-style at

Goshen College, Marion College (now Indiana Wesleyan) and in an ugly incident in Plymouth, Indiana.

Due to the housing pattern on Fort Wayne's west side, my elementary school, my junior high school and my high school were all integrated. So segregated schools had no impact on my life as a youngster. But when I began teaching across town in Fort Wayne, separate but unequal took on real meaning. It was common for a segregated school to lack adequate school materials, to have no library, no cafeteria and sometimes no gym. Segregated schools often got the "throwaways" from the white schools: discarded books, out-of-date manuals, old typewriters, inadequate supplies. My school had a faculty made up of black and white teachers who worked hard and were dedicated to the students, but the educational inequities made a level playing field impossible.

I recently found out that Linda Brown is alive and well, and has a school-age daughter attending a segregated school in Topeka, Kansas. How ironic.

Dear Linda: The more things change, the more they stay the same.

3.2

In the article she wrote in 2004 about the Brown vs. School Board Supreme Court ruling Dorothy assesses prospects for the future. The work of integrating America's schools is far from done, she says.

50 years later, there's still a lot of work to do (*Kokomo Tribune*, May 18, 2004)

Yesterday was the 50th anniversary of the historic court case pitting the Brown family versus the Topeka, Kansas School Board of Education.

Widespread and often violent resistance to the struggle for equal education for black students made the "Brown Case" an unfulfilled promise and a smoldering hope. Fifty years after the Brown Case, anti-integrationists in the North and South, along with entrenched state and federal leaders have maintained a high level of segregation in U.S. public education. And its legacy remains—poor and unequal public schools.

Segregation came into being on the heels of the Emancipation Proclamation. Segregation, a watered-down version of slavery, reshackled the black population and protected the rights and privileges of white society. Yet even at the height of segregation, there were black people who knew the promise of the 13th Amendment of the U.S. Constitution.

"Neither slavery nor involuntary servitude shall exist within the United States," the amendment reads, giving Congress the authority to write new laws.

Black people sought out the National Association for the Advancement of Colored People (NAACP) to present their oppressed condition before the U.S. court system. The NAACP legal team had very limited funds. The cases they argued before the courts had to be narrowed down to one issue at a time. And there were many issues to pick from, such as jobs, fair housing, the economy and heath care. But unequal education became the crucial focus.

It is easy to assume that the NAACP attorneys initiated the lawsuits concerning unequal public schools. Actually it was the local black people who did the necessary, such as getting signatures on petitions. The families then contacted the lawyers for their expertise. Those ordinary brave people risked their lives, jobs and homes when they signed those petitions and when they stepped forward to be plaintiffs.

At a Brown v. Board of Education anniversary ceremony, Joseph DeLaine Jr. of South Carolina spoke about how black people in his hometown suffered as a result of the Brown Case. Teacher and principals were fired from their jobs if they joined the NAACP or were suspected of being members.

Back then black high school graduates were barred from colleges and their high school records were falsified. DeLaine recounted the many verbal threats and two murders which occurred locally in the wake of the decision.

As a minister and community leader, Delaine's father was involved in the Brown case. Arsonists destroyed the DeLaine's home. The firemen came but would not put the fire out. And DeLaine Sr. could not collect on his fire insurance. He moved to a second house. It was vandalized and his church burned down. Again, arson. DeLaine Sr. was sent a letter warning him to leave town in 10 days or die. After being shot at, his father fled to New York. He died there in 1974.

DeLaine Jr. was stationed in Korea to fight for freedom for the Korean people while racist acts were being committed in his hometown and other places in the South.

Charles Hamilton Houston, Senior, a Harvard law graduate, was the lead attorney in the Brown case. He laid the complex groundwork. A professor at Howard University Law School, Houston was a key influence on future U.S. Supreme Court Justice Thurgood Marshall, who was one of Houston's top students.

Houston's philosophy of law included this belief: "In a good society the government guarantees justice and freedom for everyone while providing for succeeding generations better and broader opportunities without prejudice or bias operating against them."

When Houston died of a heart condition on April 22, 1950, his former student, Thurgood Marshall, was left with the challenging task of being the lead attorney on the Brown case.

After winning the case, Marshall, in 1961, was appointed to the U.S. Court of Appeals.

In 1965 he was appointed solicitor general of the U.S. From 1967–1991, he was the first black justice of the U.S. Supreme Court. In 2003, the postal service issued the Black Heritage Thurgood Marshall Stamp.

These two great attorneys, Houston and Marshall, led a dedicated group of lawyers who helped to make the Brown victory possible.

The team was made up of black and white attorneys. If Houston and Marshal were here today they would caution: Celebrate yes, but remember there is still unfinished work to do.

3·3

The U.S. Supreme Court had ruled that segregation is illegal. However, this ruling did not erase the deeply ingrained patterns of inequity and discrimination. As Dorothy discovered in her role as a teacher in the public schools, the devastating impact of segregation continued.

> **Unequal schools were a constant source of unrest** (*Kokomo Tribune*, March 3, 2004)
> There was very little difference between a predominantly black school "up North" and the segregated black schools in the south. I taught in a predominantly black school in Fort Wayne in the 1960s. My room was in the basement: old, drab, but clean thanks to Mr. Harding, the janitor.
> It was a struggle to get the supplies and books we needed and wanted for our students. Frank Werling, our white principal, made many appeals to the "downtown office" with limited success.
> One day I was invited to one of Fort Wayne's all-white public schools. That school had a grassy schoolyard! Inside there were adequate supplies and books, a cafeteria, a shiny-floor gym, a scoreboard that worked, murals on the wall in the brightly painted hall. Returning to my pallid basement classroom was painful and depressing. I had witnessed, firsthand, that separate is not equal.
> My friend Jayne, now a retired elementary school teacher, remembers her days in Evansville at the all-black Lincoln School in the 1950s. The teachers were dedicated and the parents were supportive. But the school had inadequate teaching materials and equipment. Jayne remembers the "throw-away" outdated books that were passed on to them from the white schools.
> Lincoln School began amidst unrest and anger from white protestors who didn't want an all-black school in their neighborhood. Nevertheless, Lincoln School, grade K-12, was built and opened in 1928. It had no cafeteria but it had a library with no books. And the school board would not allocate money for the purchase of books.

Black students from surrounding areas who wanted a high school education had to commute to Evansville's Lincoln School from such places as Mount Vernon, Rockport, Newburgh and Grandview, IN.

Fifty years ago, the U.S. Supreme Court declared an end to legal segregation, in theory ending "separate but equal" public schools. That landmark decision was known as Brown versus School Board of Education, Topeka, Kansas, 1954. The "Brown" in this case was a Mr. Oliver Brown representing his young daughter Linda Brown and several other African-American minors.

The desegregation ruling allowed school integration, and court-ordered busing was a victory for those Mr. Brown represented, but many whites responded with anger and violent acts. Some historians connect the reaction of whites to the desegregation ruling to the brutal murder of Emmett Till to the beginnings of the Civil Rights Movement. I agree. Emmett's tragic death was the spark that ignited the Civil Rights Movement, not the Montgomery Bus Boycott.

On the night of August 28, 1955, in Mississippi (barely a year after the Brown v. School Board of Education decision), Emmett Till was dragged at gun point from his great-uncle's house by two white men. He was beaten for hours, then shot in the head, then thrown into the river, a fan attached to his neck by barbed wire.

Emmet was killed because he broke a "sacred law": he whistled at a white woman. Emmett had a severe stuttering problem. He could whistle easier than he could talk. And he had just turned 14 years old. I was a teenager when Emmett was murdered, and like many thousands of people, I too mourned his death.

Back home, Emmett's body lay first at the Rayners Funeral Home in Chicago, and later in the Church of God in Christ. That Labor Day Weekend in 1955, thousands and thousands of people passed by the coffin. His mother, Mamie Till, insisted on an open coffin because it was the only way "I can tell this story" she said. Emmett's body was so damaged "he looked like something from outer space," said his mother.

In Mississippi, the two men who killed Emmett were set free after the jury deliberated for 67 minutes. Those two men later sold their story to *Look Magazine* for $4000, telling how they killed Emmett.

From time to time, I wondered whatever happened to Emmett's mother. Someone shared an article with me written by Dorothy Friesen in a publication called *The Other Side*. Friesen interviewed Mamie Till in 1991.

Mamie's strong faith helped her to cope with the trauma of losing her only child in such a cruel manner. She toured the U.S. and told her story. She worked with children and youth in the Chicago schools and in her church. She transformed her nightmare into love for all children and their possibilities, wrote Friesen.

Mamie Till Mobley died on January 6, 2003 at age 81.

3·4

Schools have the growth and welfare of children at the core of their mission. Supreme Court rulings outlawing discrimination on the basis of race eventually brought change, even though forces of resistance inevitably delayed progress. For enduring change to occur there needed to be public demonstrations of support for the education of children. Even on the cusp of her retirement from teaching Dorothy chose to demonstrate her passionate commitment to children by attending a rally in which she joined a throng of teachers and other advocates for children in the Washington Mall.

"Stand for Children" message still heard (*Kokomo Tribune,* June 4, 1997)

On June 1, 1996, over 200,000 people gathered on the Mall at the Lincoln Memorial in Washington, D.C. to participate in a "Stand for Children" Rally. Marian Wright Edelman was one of the main organizers of this demonstration, and my teacher-friend Margaret and I jumped at the chance to take part in this event. We both admire Margaret Wright Edelman, mother of three, author and founder and president of the Children's Defense Fund.

In the early hours of the rally, I had time to tour the Lincoln Memorial and recall that this was the place where Marion Anderson sang. Looking out over the reflecting pool and toward the Washington Monument I thought of King's "I Have a Dream" speech and the more recent Million Man March.

Children, women and men of many races, colors and from all stations in life were present for this upbeat occasion. It was a perfect-weather day. Margaret and I joined the thousands of people who sat on blankets under the shade trees. The program began with lots of music, instrumental and vocal, children's speeches, presentations and finally Edelman's keynote address in which she said: "Let us begin to truly stand for children. We commit ourselves to building a just America that leaves no child behind, and we commit ourselves to ensuring all our children have a healthy and safe passage to adulthood."

There were opportunities to pledge in writing to undertake some action to help improve a child's life. There was a toll free number to call for information about taking the next step.

Margaret and I were duly inspired. Margaret returned home to get ready for her third graders. I returned home, newly retired, with no prospects of child-related activities. Then I moved to Kokomo.

Most of my Kokomo friends didn't know about "Stand for Children" or my commitment, but they were great resource people. Grace encouraged me to contact Carver Center about tutoring. Sylvia handed me Book Buddy information. Anita told me about Emily's tutoring classes at Second Baptist. And Bob invited me to speak to his fourth graders at Carroll Elementary School in Flora. I "adopted" Bob's class, became a Book Buddy, and tutored nine kids.

The 1997 "Stand for Children" will not take place in Washington, D.C. this June but in one's community. This year there is an online event on the internet.

3.5

Retired teachers are no longer under contract to help children to learn but they retain memories of their years in the classroom. Many of them continue to relate to others with similar memories.

Some teachers are retired—not tired (*Kokomo Tribune*, October 25, 1997)

The place was Laughner's Cafeteria. The occasion was the fall meeting of the Howard County Retired Teacher's Association. As a transplanted retiree from Evansville, this was my first opportunity to be with this group of retired, but still energized, educators.

I learned that this group ranks community service as a high priority in reaching out and giving back. This kind of deep commitment reminded me of another retiree, Amaryllis Martin of Evansville, who is the president of the Alpha Eta Chapter of the National Sorority of the Phi Delta Kappa, Inc. actively involved in helping young people.

It is impossible to think of any retired teacher in Evansville without also remembering retiree Marye Miller Brown. Amaryllis Martin and Marye Miller Brown have a lot in common. Both are African American; both had long illustrious teaching careers; both started their careers as beginning teachers in segregated one-room schoolhouses. Marye Miller Brown was "Miss Miller" back in 1934 when she went from Indiana State Teachers College in Terra Haute to rural southwest Virginia to begin her career at one-room River Hill School. She was teacher, principal, secretary, head custodian, and fund-raiser (to help pay off the school's debt). Her salary was $40 a month. Miss Miller was assigned grades one through eight. There was no kindergarten—so she started one, the delight of the youngsters and their parents!

Her students, all African Americans, walked three miles to school each day in all kinds of weather, to the top of the hill where their school was, with its potbelly stove, low-hung ceiling, crudely-made furniture and the "outhouse" at a distance. Today, more than 60 years later, Marye Miller Brown vividly recalls that first year of teaching in the rural South as a one-of-a-kind teaching experience "I did not ever forget."

Amaryllis Martin told me that she shed many a tear at old Lyles School No. 7 in Evansville, Indiana in the 1940s. The school was so run-down and school supplies were so scarce. Everyone drank from a "common dipper" and the cloakroom was converted into a tiny kitchen where a parent cooked their meals.

Thanks to a caring teacher, students helping each other, and loyal parents, a high level of learning prevailed in that one-room school; and a student inspired by Martin as a role model is a teacher today, at Caze Elementary School in Evansville!

The last time I talked with Amaryllis Martin, she reminded me that she is retired "but not tired." The same can be said for the Howard County Retired Teachers— retired "but not tired!"

3.6

In her research into emerging strategies in education Dorothy's acute sense of cynical amusement led her to the conclusion that many of them were not as new as claimed.

Something new? 'It was here before our time' (*Kokomo Tribune*)

Modern math? Modern to whom? With those words, my summer school professor proceeded to inform us that "modern math" was not modern at all, merely packaged and marketed differently for our generation. Hearing those comforting words, I relaxed and almost enjoyed that math class!

Adult education? Modern to whom?

The newer term is Evening Classes. When I was teaching it was known as "Night School." Evening classes, night school or any kind of education was called illegal for slaves in America. However, some slaves did learn to read and write although it was clearly against the law.

Milla Granson, a slave in Kentucky, was taught reading and writing by the children of the plantation master. Upon the death of her master in Kentucky, Milla was sold to a Mississippi plantation owner. Unbeknownst to this master and his family, Milla started a school for slaves in a little cabin in a back alley. This secret school began before midnight and lasted until about two o'clock in the morning. Milla took 12 students at a time, taught them all she had learned in Kentucky, then she "graduated" them and took 12 new students.

School busing? Modern to whom?

Elfrieda V. Churchill was a kind, friendly woman who was ready to discuss almost anything except the pangs of segregation. But on one occasion, she did respond to my question about busing.

In 1928, Lincoln School, grades K-12, was the only high school for African Americans in Evansville and the surrounding cities and towns in southern Indiana. African-American students were bused to all-black Lincoln School from Mount Vernon, Rockport, Newburgh and Grandview.

Mrs. Churchill told me that when her husband was a high school student at Lincoln, he often got so engrossed in some after-school project that he'd miss the bus and have to walk home all the way to Mount Vernon! Most of Mrs. Churchill's other painful memories remained unspoken and she carried them with her to her grave, February 1, 1998.

School choice? Modern to whom?

In the 1960s, the school board in Drew, Mississippi was under court order to set up "freedom of choice" schools. Matthew and Mae Carter's seven children—Ruth, Stanley, Larry, Pearl, Gloria, Beverly and Deborah—told their parents they wanted to attend the all-white "freedom of choice" schools. Mr. and Mrs. Carter highly valued education although they themselves had never had an opportunity to get a good education.

The Carters were poor, African-American sharecroppers who willingly worked from sunrise to sunset in the cotton fields, six days a week to finance their seven children's education. All seven children progressed from elementary school to Drew High School and then to "Old Miss" University.

School Integration? Modern to whom?

In 1831, Prudence Crandall, a devout Quaker, moved from Rhode Island to Canterbury, Connecticut, to open a school for white girls at the invitation of the townspeople. Sarah Harris Fayerweather, an African American, applied for admission to the school. Miss Crandall was somewhat fearful but nevertheless admitted Sarah to the school. The townspeople were furious and refused to send their children. The school was closed. Miss Crandall then opened a school for "Young Ladies and Misses of Color." The townspeople were again outraged. A law was passed that "forbade establishing a school for colored persons." Miss Crandall had to leave the area. She moved to Kansas. But Sarah never forgot the courageous teacher who waged a futile battle on her behalf.

Sarah Fayerweather's thwarted attempt to attend an integrated place of learning was a legacy for African-Americans who followed in her footsteps—brave souls around the country and right here in Indiana who walked through school doors formerly meant for "Whites Only."

Some ancient words of wisdom declare: "There is nothing new under the sun. It was here already, long ago; it was here before our time." (Ecclesiastes 1:9–10)

3.7

As Dorothy rehearsed her teaching career she recalled first time events, both at school and in other settings, some amusing, others annoying. Her thought process leads her readers to realize that her experiences as an African American woman outside of the classroom included some dramatic and troubling events. She also illustrates with reference to a woman whose experience of being "first" was both memorable and amazing. Wilma Rudolph, raised poor, a victim of polio, overcame unbelievable obstacles to become the first African American three-time Olympic medalist.

The kind of lemonade no one wants to try (*Kokomo Tribune*, December 9, 2002)

You've probably heard the saying: "When life hands you a lemon make lemonade." If you are an African American and you are "the first" African American in a certain setting or situation, too often you get bombarded with lemons. Onlookers and bystanders are quick to say, "Just make lemonade." That's very easy for them to say since they've never had to make that much lemonade!

I was the first African-American teacher in the New Castle School System in the late 1960s. I didn't wake up one morning and decide I wanted to be the first. I simply needed a job and the principal of the school that had an opening was willing to have a black teacher on his staff.

However, the principal was nervous about my being there because he feared a reaction from the white parents with Appalachian backgrounds. Privately the principal called those parents the "Hatfields and the McCoys." But I got along well will those parents.

Nevertheless I did have some "lemon" incidents in New Castle. The most vivid one was an encounter with a white, middle-class grandmother through her grandchild in my class. Grandmother taught her first-grade granddaughter Pamela a poem one evening and Pamela was to recite that poem to me the next morning.

So, next morning, Pamela recited the words and looked at me with her innocent big blue eyes and waited for my response. I told Pamela very quietly she should share grandma's poem with the principal. Pamela went happily to the principal's office with grandma's poem fresh in her memory.

The key words of grandma's poem were: "Don't catch me, catch that n. . . behind the tree."

A more recent "lemon" incident happened when I was a newcomer to Kokomo "City of Firsts." I wanted to transfer my bank accounts from the Evansville Federal Credit Union to a Kokomo financial institution recommended to me by white Kokomo residents.

I was shocked when I was told by the bank teller and also the manager that I could not open a checking account nor a saving account with them. I was shocked even more when they asked me to transfer my IRA accounts to their bank. I wanted to know whether if I agreed to transfer my IRA accounts to their bank I would be able to open a checking or savings account with them. Again the answer was no.

Being denied banking service was a "first" for me. And even to this day I wonder what part of no they meant: No, we don't do checking or savings accounts for anyone. Or, No, we have membership rules and regulations that we won't bother to explain.

Taking a few minutes to make clear their banking policy would have been the professional bank-friendly thing to do, and would have avoided the impression that seemed to say, No, we don't want to serve you.

African Americans make up less than 20 percent of the population nationwide. In Indiana the white population is 91 percent. Do the math and you'll see that being "the first" African American in some setting or another is inevitable. Being "the first" is certainly not "pure pleasure." Too many "lemons" accompany that title.

In its spring 2002 issue, *American Legacy*, a magazine of African-American history and culture, featured the unique stories of several black women who have experienced the situation and the burden of being "the first." Wilma Rudolph was one of those women.

Wilma Rudolph was my first "shero" because Track and Field was my favorite sports event. Wilma earned her title of being "the first" at a place far from her home in Clarksville, Tennessee. The place was Rome at the 1960 Olympics. Wilma was the first black woman to win three world medals in a single Olympiad. And she is the only African American world record holder in the 200 meter race.

Wilma was the first African American to receive the National Sports award, but there were many other awards as well.

In spite of her untimely death in 1993, Wilma has left a shining example of courage and perseverance and of overcoming obstacles. Being born poor, black, and then being disabled with polio at age four, and practically immobile until age 12 would have overwhelmed the average person.

With the love and support of family and friends, Wilma was not stopped in her tracks. Slowly she regained the ability to walk, then the ability to run. Once she started running she never stopped. And the rest is history!

3.8

In 1962 Dorothy earned her B.A. in Education at Marion College (now Indiana Wesleyan University). However she had begun her college studies at Goshen College. In her columns she makes occasional references to her experiences as an African American woman on these campuses. Two of her articles deal specifically with initiatives taken at Goshen College toward becoming more inclusive and accepting of students of color. Here is one of them.

The face of Goshen College has changed in 42 years
(*Kokomo Tribune*, July 18, 1998)

Eighty-three year old Dr. John Hope Franklin is cautiously optimistic about the future of race relations in America. He has seen some positive changes in race relations in his lifetime but "not nearly enough." Dr. Franklin heads President Clinton's Initiative on Race— One America in the 21st Century campaign, which was announced in June 1997. Colleges and universities were asked by the president to lead the way in establishing community dialogue on race issues.

My June issue of the *GC Bulletin* tells about Goshen College students, faculty and administrators working with the complex challenge of race on campus and in the community. Zenebe Abebe, vice president for multi-cultural education at Goshen College, said, "When students graduate and go into the work force, there is a greater chance than ever before that they'll have a supervisor who is of a different ethnic background, or they will supervise someone of another culture. They will need to respond to that person and learn to make comfortable relationships."

Goshen College is leading the way in encouraging curriculum enrichment and offering a variety of innovative programs. "We find we are at the cutting edge of offering students the opportunity to learn in a multicultural environment," said Abebe. "Faculty, administration and staff members have been very supportive of the efforts of the office, and our goal is to continue."

The pro-diversity stance is quite a contrast to the Goshen College I experienced as one of the few African-Americans on that campus in the 1950s. Some of the administrators, faculty and staff I encountered were ambivalent at best, while others deemed their rebuffs, slights and insensitive remarks to be for my own good, saddling me with the double burden of coping with the offenses and the offenders.

The good news is that most of the white students I had contact with were not ambivalent or hesitant about being friendly. However, when I left the Goshen campus, I vowed never to return. But in the fall of 1997, my foremost friend from those college days, Grace Sommers Whitehead, persuaded me to attend the Ethnic Fair at Goshen College. The Fair was a festive celebration of diversity, an event unthinkable in my college days!

As we drove into Goshen, Indiana, my eyes drank in the small-town surroundings for the very first time. As an African American student in the 1950s, this town was off-limits to me. Undeniably, the town and the college have come a long way over the 42 year span from my freshman days to this summer of 1998. And the theme of my June *GC Bulletin*, "Working at Racism" detailing the college's leadership and the town's cooperation, gives me cause to be cautiously optimistic about the future of race relations.

I PONDER. . .

Both Dorothy and I chose to pursue careers in education, she in elementary school in Indiana and I in high schools in Saskatchewan and Manitoba. After three years my path took me on a detour into pastoral ministry and then graduate level teaching at Anabaptist Mennonite Biblical Seminary. I wish that I had sought opportunities for the two of us, together with other teachers, to recall our teaching experiences and reflect on them, especially as pertaining to racial, gender, and economic equality of access to an education.

My conversation with Dorothy, and hopefully also a group of culturally and ethnically diverse partners, might have started with our personal narratives.

- As a child in elementary school Dorothy was featured in a newspaper article as an exemplary student. My name regularly appeared in the *Valley News* along with other students on the annual honor roll. Is this kind of recognition helpful for a child?

- Despite being raised in a religiously and culturally conservative family system where education requirements were resisted or grudgingly accepted I declared at a young age that I would become a teacher. And I persisted in pursuing that vocational goal. If I had been born into a poor, black family, what would it have taken for me to succeed in this pursuit? What barriers did you face in your pursuit of an education?

- The history of segregated schools as one expression of deeply rooted patterns of exclusion based on race does not evoke comparable memories for me.

- Dorothy recalls that as a student at Goshen College in the 1950s the discomfort she felt on campus was exacerbated by the fact that the city of Goshen was a sundown town where blacks were required to leave before dark. How does this make you feel now?

4

Heritage

NARRATIVES AND ANECDOTES ABOUT Black experience in America appear repeatedly in Dorothy's writings. Her articles pass on the heritage that undergirds life in the interconnected community of mutual support, the Village. Already in her paradigmatic article featured in chapter 1, Dorothy asserts that "African Americans were birthed, nurtured, role-modeled, encouraged, supported and applauded in the Village." She also emphasizes the extensive and inclusive character of the Village, "encircling domestics and doctors; beauticians and bankers; teachers and TV hosts; singers and scientists; preachers and politicians; authors and actors; and all African Americans striving toward the 21st century."

Each year, beginning in 2016, Lillian and I wrote Christmas letters to Dorothy's friends and family. We always included a photo that featured Dorothy but usually also included one or both of us. We always longed to include a greeting and personal message from Dorothy but that was no longer possible. In a letter written on December 7, 2017 we decided to include a summation of the values and commitments that had guided her in the past. I share a paragraph from that letter:

What might Dorothy share with you if she were able? We know from our earlier experiences with her and the conversations we've had with some of you that she was a gifted woman committed to sharing the Gospel of peace, compassion, and justice in our world. This is corroborated by the columns she wrote for the *Kokomo Tribune* and the solicitation letters that she continues to receive from various charities that she supported in the past. So, I imagine that Dorothy would greet you warmly and give witness to her longing that all people would be treated equally and with genuine acceptance. And arising in part out of her own personal struggles she would challenge all of us to be people moved by compassion for the poor, the hurting and the marginalized.

When I was crafting this precis of Dorothy's heart of compassion for the marginalized I presumed that her preferential stance was shaped in part by her own struggles, both in her personal life and in her vocation as a teacher. I often wondered to what extent she was aware of the story of her ancestral family. I pondered what kind of impact that story had on her. In my letters to her friends and family I solicited memories and testimonials. The responses I received did not include family history going back to past generations. I chose to become more explicit in my request. The following is an excerpt:

> I write to follow up on a matter that I have discussed with each of you, namely my book-in-process with a collection of Dorothy's articles. In her columns Dorothy frequently referred to Black Heritage Stamps and black athletes, scientists, and reformers whose contributions have often been undervalued. Dorothy refers to slavery, emancipation, segregation, and the struggle for civil rights. I wish now that I had invited her when she was still well to tell me what she knew about her own family history during these difficult stages of the still ongoing struggle for rights and equality. What do you know about this part of Dorothy's personal and family story? I hope you feel free to reply.

Responses to this request have been slow in coming in.

Dorothy did have ways to communicate what she considered to be important expressions of her heritage as an African American woman living in America. Visitors appearing at the door of Dorothy's apartment in the assisted living wing of Waterford Crossing were typically greeted by what resembled a classroom bulletin board. Posted on it were photos or newspaper clippings or children's art, all chosen to fit within a particular social or historical theme. The items she chose for Women's History Month (for example) tended to be displayed again in March a year later, along with additional materials that she had collected in the meantime. Other themes featured on her doorway bulletin board included: Civil Rights Champions; Martin Luther King Jr Day; Mother's Day and Father's Day; Thanksgiving; Christmas; Kwanzaa. Articles transcribed below enlarge on these and other themes that she deemed significant in recalling and continuing the African American heritage.

DOROTHY'S WORD

Children growing up in African American homes learn that they have inherited the fruit of the relentless quest of creative and dedicated ancestors to make life better for themselves and others. Such children are also invited to envision themselves as having the potential to contribute to the betterment of many people. The creativity, ingenuity, and selfless search for solutions to healthcare problems and challenges in many other areas of life can characterize their contributions as well.

4.1

When Dorothy recalls the African American heritage she often includes stories of scientists and engineers whose inventions have dramatically improved the quality of life for many people around the world. An example that Dorothy cites is Otis Boykin, an electronic scientist who had 26 patents to his credit. The pace-maker is one of them; it releases low-energy electrical impulses to the heart to keep it beating at the appropriate rate and rhythm.

Passing the Torch (*Kokomo Tribune*, January 20, 2004)

I have a book published shortly after the assassination of President John Kennedy on November 22, 1963. The title of this very special book, *The Torch has Passed*, comes from a passage in the President's inaugural address on January 20, 1961, 43 years ago. "Let the word go forth, from this time and place, to friend and foe alike, that the torch has passed to a new generation of Americans."

Probably the most popular passing of the torch is the Olympic torch. That lighted torch is brought from the valley of Olympia, Greece, where the ancient original Olympics began in 776 B.C. Passing the torch begins four weeks before the start of the Olympic Games in the host country.

Thousands of relay runners take part in passing the Olympic torch, each running a certain distance. In our modern times, planes and ships transport the torch across mountains and seas, then runners carry the torch toward its final destination. Traditionally the last runner carries the lighted torch into the stadium, circles the track and lights the Olympic Flame.

Passing the torch is an important symbolic ritual, a sacred tradition in many cultures, societies and special groups. Older generations have been faithful in passing on values, family traditions and their wisdom to the "new generation."

There have been some very productive but not well-known African Americans who passed the torch and benefitted people all around the world. Dr. Charles Drew was one of those "torch passers."

Dr. Drew was an African American doctor who through his research on blood plasma in the 1930s-1940s discovered that plasma has a longer shelf life than whole blood. With that knowledge he set up blood bank programs. Drew headed up the Emergency Plasma Program for England during World War II.

When the U.S. entered the war, Drew was chosen to head the National Blood Bank Program, later called the American Red Cross Blood Bank. He and his associates developed standardized methods for banking blood and shipping plasma oversees. The plasma collected by blood banks for blood transfusions saved millions of lives during and also after the war.

In the 1940s and during World War II the Red Cross maintained segregated blood banks. Whites were given blood from white donors, African Americans were given blood from black donors.

By the 1950s, the war was over but segregation was not. That year, Dr. Drew was in a serious car accident. He needed blood. He was taken to a hospital but he was not admitted because he was black. This man who established the first blood banks and saved many lives bled to death. He was 46 years old.

Althea Gibson was a "torch-passer" who passed the "tennis torch" to African Americans who would be inspired to grab that torch and go forward to accomplish even bigger and better things than she could foresee.

Althea Gibson was the first African American to play tennis at Forest Hills (USA) in 1950; and in 1951 the first African American to play at Wimbledon, England. In 1957 she played at Wimbledon again, this time winning the Singles Championship, and received personal congratulations from Queen Elizabeth.

Gibson faced hostile tennis fans and a segregated public that wanted to keep tennis an all-white sport. Like Gibson, the sisters Venus and Serena Williams, 21st century tennis champions, face the same kind of hostility. But they bounce back from the booing crowds and sportscasters and sports writers who make no effort to be fair and balanced in their comments.

The Williams sisters have won singles titles, the double crowns, the U.S. Open, at Wimbledon and at the Olympics—holding up high the torch passed to them.

These young ladies know that there is life after tennis and are pursuing business careers. Serena Williams has been designing her own clothing line Aneres (her name spelled backwards). Her sister Venus designs clothing for the Wilson Leather stores.

Whether we are the older generation or the "new generation" we all have a torch to pass on or carry. Torches are not just for the rich and famous. All our torches together can shed some light, ignite a flame or just make life a little better.

Will we say, "Let the word go forth, from this time and place, to friend and foe alike" so that our collective torches will make our little corner of the world the best it can be? And we'll do more in 2004. It is up to us. Question: Are we up to it?

4.2

Dorothy frequently tells about women who fought for the vulnerable and the violated. An article that she wrote for Women's History Month features a civil rights activist who advocated for children and a journalist who exposed the widespread practice of lynching.

Thoughts on two women who made a difference (*Kokomo Tribune*, March 4, 2003)
An enthusiastic group called the National History Project led a coalition that successfully lobbied Congress to designate the month of March as Women's History Month.

This took place in the 1980s, and the Congressional Resolution stated: "American women of every culture, class and ethnic background have made historic contributions to the growth and strength of our nation in countless recorded and unrecorded ways."

Too bad March has only 31 days! That's not nearly enough time to adequately tell the stories of women who have done, and women that are still doing extraordinary things. Their historic contributions touch the most important segments of American life.

Marian Wright Edelman would probably insist that she's just an ordinary woman—a preacher's daughter, a wife, mother, grandmother and a professional woman. She's all that, and more.

Lawyer Edelman began a passionate crusade in behalf of poor, disadvantaged children in the 1960s. Her dedicated efforts in this area led her to start the Children's Defense Fund. As president and founder of this national advocacy organization Edelman championed children's issues. She fought for Head Start and other welfare and health care programs for the poor.

"We will not be a strong country unless we invest in every one of our children," she said. She wanted the White House and Congress sensitized to the fact that the poor and their children have needs like everyone else. And she insisted that "no American child will be left behind."

Do these words sound familiar? "No child left behind" were Edelman's words that politicians grabbed and used over and over again as if they had invented them.

Edelman's powerful, poignant words—leave no child behind—were in her heart and mind and in her book, *The Measure of our Success—A Letter to my Children and Yours*, published in 1992.

The book is filled with wisdom she shares with her three sons about the mothering she gave them at the same time not ignoring other people's children who were in greater need. The book's centerpiece, "Twenty-five lessons for life" is an open letter to all of America from this extraordinary mother.

On June 1, 1996, there were 200,000 people on the mall at Lincoln Memorial in Washington, D.C. I was there too! She was the keynote speaker. "We commit ourselves to building a just America that leaves no child behind." Those familiar words were assurance that her fight for poor, disadvantaged children was still going strong.

I was in Philadelphia, April 2002, when I heard Edelman speak to 10,000 women at the United Methodist Women's Assembly. Again, Edelman urged, "Leave no child behind." We agreed to do our part.

There are thousands of women who, in their quiet way, have made significant contributions to this nation but we will never know their names. Their wonderful deeds have gone unrecorded, lost history.

Fortunately Ida B. Wells, a teacher turned newspaper publisher, left some recorded history that shows her efforts to stop bad laws and violent public practices, efforts to make a positive difference in this country.

Ida was born a slave in Holly Springs, Mississippi, near the end of the Civil War. Yellow Fever killed her parents and baby brother. Then Jim Crow laws, segregation and lynchings, especially the lynching of her friends put her in a world of terror.

Ida started her own newspaper, *Memphis Free Speech*, to expose the violent horrible happenings. But freedom isn't free. It comes at a high price and Ida learned that truth when her newspaper office was destroyed by fire. Ida moved to New York and continued her anti-lynching efforts.

In 1892, when lynching was at its peak, Ida wrote a book, *Southern Horrors: Laws in all its Phases*. In 1895 she wrote another book, *The Red Book*. It gave extensive accounts of the thousands of men, women and, yes, children lynched after the Civil War. Also she documented the lynchings of black soldiers who had returned home after serving in WWI.

Ida married, had four children, then grandchildren, but she still found time—indeed made time—to work on anti-lynching campaigns until her death in 1931.

4.3

One of Dorothy's articles compares the U.S. national anthem, "Oh, say can you see" with what came to be known during the civil rights era as the Black National Anthem: "Lift every voice and sing." Its lyrics narrate the legacy of slavery and the struggle for freedom.

Negro national anthem one of those best kept secrets
(*Kokomo Tribune*, January 18, 2000)

Suppose you went to a ball game and the announcer said, "Please stand and sing the Negro national anthem,

'Lift every voice and sing.'" Would you have to ask, "What song is that?" If so, you wouldn't be the only one asking, because the Negro national anthem is one of those best kept secrets. And it was written 100 years ago.

PBS's "The American Experience—America 1900" depicts the beginning of the 20th century as a time when most Americans were feeling very positive about the country, and there was a "can do" spirit among the people. Many African Americans, while no longer slaves yet not fully free, nevertheless got caught up in the heady optimism of that time.

In that setting of promising possibilities in 1900, poet James Weldon Johnson penned:

Lift every voice and sing, till earth and heaven ring,
Ring with the harmonies of liberty;
Let our rejoicing rise, high as the listening skies,
Let it resound loud as the rolling sea.

And those words became the first verse of the Negro national anthem.

About 100 years earlier, another poet, Francis Scott Key, wrote "The Star-Spangled Banner" ("Oh, say can you see. . .") during the War of 1812. But his song did not reach its full popularity until the 20th century when Congress adopted it as the nation's national anthem in 1931.

Besides being two great songs of the 20th century, "Lift Every Voice and Sing" and "The Star-Spangled Banner" have something else in common. Both are musically difficult to sing. I have heard complaints about how hard it is to sing, "Oh, say can you see." Some critics want the tune simplified.

"Lift every voice and sing" was first sung in Jacksonville, Florida, at a special celebration. An all-black chorus of school children sang the three very long and musically complex verses.

Later on, segregated black schools and black churches in the South sang the anthem regularly. When African Americans migrated from the South to other parts of the country, they took "Lift every voice and sing," the Negro national anthem, with them.

I first heard this momentous song at a gathering "up North." Later I heard it at award banquets; after that, at black history celebrations and Kwanzaa festivities.

This anthem acknowledges the legacy of slavery; it also embraces the present and looks to the future.

Stony the road we trod, bitter the chastening rod,
Felt in the days when hope unborn had died.
We have come over a way that with tears has been watered,
Treading our path through the blood of the slaughtered;
Out from the gloomy past, till now we stand at last.
Sing a song full of the faith that the dark past has taught us,
Sing a song full of the hope that the present has brought us;
Facing the rising sun of our new day begun,
Let us march on till victory is won.

If Francis Scott King could "come back and walk the earth" would he be pleased or shocked and amused by the people who have attempted to sing "The Star-Spangled Banner" at public events? Perhaps he would agree with me that Whitney Houston has been the best singer of "Oh, Say can you see."

And if James Weldon Johnson could return to earth he might be pleasantly surprised that his 100-year old song is still being sung in this new century by many people who gladly "lift every voice and sing."

4.4

Among the African American memorabilia regularly mounted adjacent to the entry into Dorothy's room were displays featuring commemorative stamps issued by the U.S. Postal Service. In an article published in 2003 she offers brief bios of several of the 26 people recognized in this annual release of Black Heritage Stamps.

Bringing back the past through Black Heritage stamps
(*Kokomo Tribune*, Feb. 18, 2003)

When I lived in New Castle 26 years ago, there was a Caucasian man living there who was guilty of "random acts of kindness." His name was Miles Marshall. And I was a recipient of one of Marshall's acts of kindness.

One day on a trip to the local post office Marshall discovered something new. The post office was selling the first in a series of Black Heritage Stamps—"person stamps" to honor African Americans.

Perhaps Marshall thought I would like some of those first issue historic stamps. He was absolutely right. And thanks to Marshall I have been collecting Black Heritage Stamps ever since that day.

The Black Heritage Stamp series began in 1977 with one African American being honored each year. Twenty six have been honored as of February 2003. Some well-known personalities who have been honored in this historic series include Martin Luther King, Jackie Robinson, former Supreme Court Justice Thurgood Marshall (on this year's Black Heritage Stamp), and Malcolm X. Yes, Malcolm X!

I was as surprised as anyone that the post office issued a stamp of Malcolm X because Malcolm X was considered a controversial person. Truth be told, Martin Luther King was also considered a controversial figure when he was alive. King did not become a beloved and much-quoted American icon until long after his death.

Black Heritage Stamp no.1 of Harriet Tubman leads the way. How fitting, because Tubman led the way many times during her lifetime. She was famous for leading more than 300 slaves to freedom. Tubman was well-known as "the Moses of her People" as she successfully led them Up North and even into Canada through a series of hiding places provided by white abolitionists and free blacks: hiding places called "the Underground Railroad."

Black Heritage Stamp no. 16 honored Dr. Percy L. Julian, a renowned research chemist. Dr. Julian's scientific research should be appreciated by everyone who has glaucoma or arthritis or muscular discomfort. Dr. Julian was a research chemist at DePauw University in Greencastle in 1932. In the chemistry lab Julian succeeded in synthesizing physostigmine, the drug used in treating glaucoma.

Dr. Julian's biggest achievement occurred when he was the leading research chemist at the Glidden

Company in Chicago. He discovered how to extract white crystals called sterols from soybean oil. From sterols he produced Compound S—from which synthetic cortisone could be made and could be manufactured commercially at a price people could afford.

On September 12, 1992, Dr. Mae Jemison, a Chicago physician, was the first black woman to venture into outer space as one of the seven-member crew aboard the space shuttle Endeavor. But Bessie Coleman, Black Heritage Stamp no. 18, was "in the air" long before Mae Jamison was born! Coleman was the first licensed African American pilot (1921).

She was trained in France because no American flight school would accept blacks. Upon her return to America in 1922, "Brave Bessie" thrilled the crowds with her barnstorming flights. She also gave lectures in black schools and churches and was an inspiration to the young people. A 12-year-old girl wrote a letter to Coleman, "I like to see our race do brave things."

Langston Hughes was on last year's Black Heritage Stamp no. 25. He was honored as one of America's great African American poets. His poem, "I, too, sing America," written so long ago, is very up to date. "I, too, sing America. I am the darker brother" reminds me of the unnoticed, unacknowledged patriotism of African Americans in spite of being buffeted with unchanged indignities from "way back then."

My father served in France during World War I. He returned home to even more Jim Crow laws. My brother returned from Korea and endured segregation wrath when he drank at the wrong water fountain. My great-nephew returned from Desert Storm to target racial profiling. Another great-nephew is in Kuwait right now. If he survives Kuwait, I wonder what's in store for him when he "comes marching home again."

Twenty-six Black Heritage Stamps and 26 years later, I am wondering whatever happened to that kind man, Miles Marshall. Is he still doing "random acts of kindness"? I'll have to ask my friends who live in New Castle. They know everything!

4.5

Black athletes often appear in Dorothy's anecdotal narration of contributions made by African Americans to the fabric of American culture. In their pursuit of opportunities to compete on a level playing field alongside white athletes they demonstrated dogged perseverance and resilience in the face of discriminatory actions against them. As a sports fan herself, Dorothy exhibits her pride in the accomplishments of athletes in a variety of sports. The baseball player whose prowess elicits Dorothy's special admiration is Jackie Robinson.

> **"Baseball" told the real story** (*Kokomo Tribune*, April 16, 1997)
> My apologies to filmmaker Ken Burns for pre-judging his documentary, "Baseball." This happened a few years ago when I heard that "Baseball" was going to be shown on PBS. I was skeptical and wondered what there was to be said about baseball that would take nine episodes/innings? I found out posthaste as Burns retold American history through the vehicle of baseball, lime lighting little-known facts about African American baseball in the pre-Jackie Robinson era.
> Like most Americans, I thought Robinson was the first African American to integrate major league baseball. But watching Ken Burns' "Baseball" I learned that from 1884 to 1887 African Americans played in the major leagues alongside white baseball players. Then in 1887 the "Gentleman's Agreement" among white club owners caused the disappearance of African Americans from the major leagues for 60 years.
> During the 60 years the "Gentleman's Agreement" was in effect, African American baseball players had a league of their own. Their 140-game schedule was exciting and competitive with Baseball Hall of Fame caliber players and outstanding, entertaining teams like: the Indianapolis Clowns, Chicago American Giants, Louisville Cubs, Newark Eagles, Pittsburgh Crawfords, and the Kansas City Monarchs. Robinson played for the

Monarchs before going to the Dodgers farm team and then to the major leagues.

Jackie Robinson was my No. 1 hero and the Brooklyn Dodgers was my most favorite team. Branch Rickey, president and general manager of the Dodgers, was a public relations man in a class all by himself. On April 15, 1947, Rickey put Robinson in the starting lineup as first baseman, an historic act designed to put an end to the "Gentleman's Agreement," reopening league baseball to African Americans. Rickey also knew that including this formerly excluded one-tenth of the population would significantly boost major league baseball revenues.

Most fans, myself included, had no idea what price Robinson paid to play for the Dodgers. Burns' meticulous research revealed the "fine print" in Jackie Robinson's contract which stipulated that for three years Robinson could not respond or react to any abuse he received from his teammates, from other teams and their owners, or from hostile fans. So, for three long years, Robinson endured non-stop racial slurs, threats of being shot from the stands, written and phoned threats to him and his family; plus being thrown at by pitchers and spiked by base runners. Robinson fulfilled his contract to the letter while leading the Dodgers in home runs and being named Rookie of the Year.

Ken Burns' documentary covered the whole spectrum of baseball, not just white versus black issues; but exposing those aspects of baseball history was crucial in making the story complete.

After watching all nine innings of Burns' "Baseball" I consider this documentary a real hit—a three balls two strikes, bottom of the ninth grand slam!

4.6

As she remembers contributions made by African Americans toward the quality of life for all people, regardless of cultural status and ethnicity, she recalls some whose life was prematurely cut short by illness or accident. She thinks about scientists whose medical research produced long term results. An award-winning playwright comes to her mind. She remembers a professional tennis player who achieved greatness on the world stage. What all might these three have achieved had they lived longer?

Death often comes too early to those who achieve greatness (*Kokomo Tribune*, 1997)

I was channel grazing, flipping through the different networks. I paused momentarily on one station where Toni Braxton was in the middle of some mournful melancholy song with lyrics that repeated: "Gone too soon... Gone too soon."

I don't know the intent of the song writer or what the message was. But it made me think how those words rang true for at least three African Americans I greatly admire who have indeed gone too soon.

I remember Dr. Charles Richard Drew with gratitude; a man whose life-saving idea continues to save lives everywhere.

Drew headed up the Emergency Plasma Program for England during World War II. When the U.S. entered the war, Drew was chosen to head the National Blood Bank Program, later called the American Red Cross Blood Bank. He was uniquely qualified for this job. During his internship and residency at Montreal General Hospital, Drew developed an interest in the problems of sharing blood for transfusions. Later, at Columbia University's College of Physicians and Surgeons, he entered a Doctor of Science Degree program for his research into the use of stored blood plasma for shock.

In 1950, Drew, the man who established the first blood banks, bled to death because he was in a car crash and was refused admittance to the hospital because of his race. He was 46 years old.

For me, Lorraine Hansberry's highly acclaimed play "A Raisin in the Sun" was riveting and heart-wrenching—more than just entertainment.

In 1959, Hansberry received New York's Drama Critics Circle Award for the best play of the season. "A Raisin in the Sun" ran for 19 month on Broadway. Columbia Pictures bought the movie rights and hired

Hansberry to write the movie script. The film won the Cannes Film Festival Award.

Hansberry was about 27 years old when she wrote this play, soon followed by "The Sign in Sidney Brustein Window" and "Laughing Boy."

Hansberry was working on an opera when she became ill and died of cancer at age 35.

Grace and dignity rank high in my values system. Arthur Ashe had both.

Born and reared in Richmond, Virginia, Ashe made history for nearly 30 years, beginning in 1963 when he joined the U.S. Davis Cup Team as its first African American tennis player until his untimely death in February 1993. At his peak, Ashe was ranked #1 in the world of men's professional tennis.

Ashe also authored several books. *Days of Grace* was his last book. In it he tells of how he dealt with the medical blunder that caused him to get AIDS; the life-long struggle with racism; and tender touching words to his wife, Jeanne, and daughter, Camera Elizabeth.

In July, 1996, in Richmond, Virginia a monument was dedicated to Arthur Ashe. It stands on a boulevard line with statues of Confederate heroes: Arthur Ashe (1943–1993).

With life expectancy now into the late 80s, I often wonder what other contributions these three people would have made to America—and to the world—had they not "gone too soon."

Editor's note: I have not consistently fact checked Dorothy's writings. In this case I did, and I discovered that apparently what she says about how Dr. Charles Richard Drew died relies on hearsay. (cf. also in article cited on p. 79) A biographical overview published in the *National Library of Medicine* under "The Charles R. Drew papers" attempts to set the record straight:

Drew died on April 1, 1950, in Burlington, North Carolina, from injuries sustained in a car accident while en route to a conference. Despite the prompt and consistent care he received from the white physicians at a nearby hospital, he was too badly injured to survive. Drew's

tragic death generated a persistent myth that he died
because he was denied admission to the white hospital,
or was denied a transfusion, but such stories have been
debunked repeatedly. Though he died prematurely, Drew
left a substantial legacy, embodied in his blood bank
work and especially in the graduates of the Howard University School of Medicine.[1]

4.7

Dorothy calls to mind the heritage of other African American heroes as well, including scientists and inventors. She laments that
when people think about the collective identity of the United States
they typically ignore the fact that many Americans are not white.

> **Say 'American' and you visualize a white person** (*Ko-
> komo Tribune*, April 1, 2003)
>
> This happened a few years ago before I retired. I
> don't remember whether we were going to or coming
> from an after-school meeting. I don't remember how
> many of us were riding in the van. What I do remember
> is the anger directed at me because I used the hyphen-
> ated word "African-American."
>
> The teacher driving the van erupted and exclaimed,
> "Why can't we all just call ourselves Americans?"
>
> I've heard that heated question asked by whites
> many times since that day. And the answer remains the
> same. Say "American" and you automatically visualize a
> white person.
>
> For example, examine this short list of American
> inventors: Meredith Gourdine, Norbert Rillieux, Jan E.
> Matzeliger and Sarah E. Goode. Ninety-nine percent
> of Americans—red, brown, yellow, black and white—
> would automatically assume that those inventors were
> white. Actually they were African-American inventors.
> So to give credit where credit is due, hyphenated names
> are necessary.

1. "Biographical Overview," para. 12 (https://profiles.nlm.nih.gov/
spotlight/bg/feature/biographical-overview).

Imitating the style of the TV show Jeopardy: Leo
Gertstenzang invented the Q-tip, Ole Evenrude invented
the outboard motor and Charles Strite invented the automatic toaster. Question: What are the three white inventors who produced these very useful inventions?

Next category: African-American inventors: Garrett A. Morgan, Elijah McCoy and Otis Boykin.

Morgan invented the earliest type of gas mask in
1912, an airtight canvas hood connected to a special
breathing tube. It was an effective inhalator, the forerun-
ner of the modern gas mask. In 1916, Morgan used his
gas mask to rescue more than 20 workers trapped in a
smoke-filled sunken tunnel shaft beneath Lake Erie. The
city of Cleveland awarded a gold medal to Morgan for his
heroic deed. But Moran was plagued with nightmarish
memories of that tunnel disaster until his death at age
86, in 1963.

Police department and fire departments nationwide
bought Morgan's gas mask but some canceled their order
when they learned that Morgan was African-American.

During the Desert Storm War not only troops but
also civilians had to put on gas masks. During that war
a camera man filmed a mother struggling to put a min-
iature gas mask on her young frightened child, a very
sad sight. The people in that village were anticipating a
missile attack.

Think of Garrett Morgan also as you wait at a traffic
light. He invented the first automatic traffic signal. It had
stop-and-go arms which systematically raised and low-
ered. Another model had red, yellow and green lights.
Eventually, Morgan sold the rights to his invention to
General Electric for $40,000.

Elijah McCoy's inventions were very important and
greatly appreciated in the world of mechanical engineer-
ing. That is not my world. Nevertheless, I was curious
and wanted to find out the origin of the expression, "The
Real McCoy."

It began with McCoy's first invention—an auto-
mated device that self-lubricated moving parts on trains
and other machines. McCoy studied mechanical engi-
neering in Scotland, but back in America he worked as

a fireman on several trains. His job was to oil the trains' moving parts—after the trains stopped.

Performing that task sparked the idea that led to McCoy's invention of the lubricating cup that could continuously supply lubricant to moving parts of machines. Thanks to McCoy, machines didn't have to be stopped anymore in order to be oiled. The phrase "The Real Mc-Coy" probably originated with the machinery buyers who insisted that their new equipment have only McCoy lubricators.

Inventor Otis Boykin was an electronic scientist who had 26 patents. One of his 26 inventions was the electrical resistor used in many computers, radios, television sets and other electronically controlled devices like guided missiles. But Boykin's best known invention, the control unit for an artificial heart stimulator, is also called a pacemaker. This device is inserted into the body to deliver small regular shocks to stimulate the heart to beat in a normal rhythm.

"A pacemaker saved my life," a friend told me. "Well," I warned, "stay away from microwaves." My friend informed me that microwaves are not a problem anymore. And now you can have your pacemaker checked and listened to over the phone! At airports, however, you still need to tell the authorities that you are wearing a pacemaker, she said.

Blacks have been inventing things from slavery times to now, but there are no African-American inventors in the National Inventors Hall of Fame—in spite of all the contributions they have made to American daily life.

I PONDER. . .

When I visit our public library I typically head first to the new books shelf. When a title catches my attention I remove it from the shelf and examine the inside back cover. If I discover that the author is Black I tend to react with an element of surprise. The author's name does not signal racial identity, and my presumption is that the skin tone of the writer must be like mine.

I am accustomed to seeing TV coverage of black athletes excelling on a football or basketball court, but when I see a black woman in medical garb caring for a patient my initial instinct is often surprise.

I admit that I often assume that my champions are racially similar to me. In a conversation with African American colleagues, ideally in a racially diverse group, I would like to share about my instinctive assumptions. Perhaps my conversation partners will feel free to share theirs.

Having read Dorothy's articles about African Americans whose legacy includes inventions, medical research, national anthems, athletic prowess, and literature we might try to list some of them and then develop a parallel list of white Americans with comparable achievements.

What do you notice?

5

Dream

THE TITLE OF ONE of Dorothy's articles says it all: "They killed the dreamer, but the dream lives on." (*Kokomo Tribune*, January 12, 2000) African Americans inspired by their heritage to persist in the quest for justice are sustained by the dream of a hopeful future marked by peace, inclusion, and wholeness. Activists, prophets, and visionaries of all ethnic groups and from all nations longed for this dream increasingly to become reality in the midst of adversity. Both those who now enjoy name recognition and the anonymous faithful further back in the crowd have been, and continue to be, champions in the parade moving into a future with hope. Many have also been cheerleaders affirming these champions and urging them to carry on with courage and resilience.

Dorothy had a small collection of children's books on the modest shelf in her room. One book is by Desmond Tutu, *God's Dream*. Dorothy could no longer read it herself but when we read it to her she was always keenly attentive, especially since the artist's illustrations all featured children. Imagining a child sitting next to Dorothy reading this book inspired us to realize that she continued to be moved by the Dream. Both the introduction and the conclusion of this book begin with the words, "Dear child of God";

> Dear child of God, What do you dream about in your loveliest of dreams?
> Do you dream about flying high or rainbows reaching across the sky?
> Do you dream about being free to do what your heart desires?
> Or about being treated like a full person no matter how young you might be?
> Do you know what God dreams about?
> Dear child of God, do you know how to make God's dream come true?
> It is really quite easy.
> As easy as sharing, loving, caring.
> As easy as holding, playing, laughing.
> As easy as knowing we are family because we are all God's children.
> Will you help God's dream come true?
> Let me tell you a secret . . .
> God smiles like a rainbow when you do.[1]

DOROTHY'S WORD

Repeated reminders of racial discrimination experienced by African Americans and other people of color in the United States provide the backdrop for the contrasting theme of hope. Within the ongoing struggle for justice and equality there have always been voices of hope. Indeed, the Dream lives on! The following articles highlight the vision for a hopeful future spoken and enacted by advocates of the Dream.

Articles in Dorothy's repertoire articulated the dream and pointed to individuals and groups that sought to embody the dream. It is not surprising that in January, when the U.S. celebrates Martin Luther King Jr. Day, Dorothy prominently features civil

1. Desmond Tutu and Douglas Carlton Abrams, *God's Dream* (Cambridge, MA: Candlewick, 2008), pp. 1–5 and 24–30.

rights leaders who persistently demonstrated against discrimination and acted for justice.

5.1

Considering the dreamers who acted in line with their dreams, Dorothy notes patterns. She cites James Lawson, who mentored Martin Luther King, and John Lewis, who marched with King in Selma, Alabama and then continued to advocate for the dream in the House of Representatives. They were willing to forgive their opponents, and they pursued nonviolent responses to hatred and discrimination.

> **Admiration for those who believe nonviolence** (*Kokomo Tribune*, January 15, 1999)
>
> Alexander Pope wrote: "To err is human, to forgive is divine." Human error is pretty common. But to forgive, to really forgive, is not so common. James Lawson is a man who truly knows how to forgive. He has lived it, inspired it, taught it, and helped to change America because of it.
>
> James Lawson grew up in Ohio. When he was 11 years old he slapped a white boy who called him a nasty name. When James told his mother about it she talked to him about Christian love. From then, for the rest of his life, he committed himself to a life of genuine forgiveness in dealing with hate, anger, aggression and other despicable acts from his attackers.
>
> Lawson's lifestyle took on the form of conscientious objection during the Korean War. He served 14 months in jail for that decision. Upon his release he went to India as a Methodist missionary. While in India, Lawson learned the teaching of Mohandas Gandhi, how Gandhi led his people to reshape India "without raising so much as a fist."
>
> When Lawson returned to America in 1956 he enrolled at Oberlin College to study theology. In 1957 Martin Luther King visited Oberlin to make a speech. There the two men met for the first time. While the

media chose to focus their attention on Martin Luther King, Lawson remained in relative obscurity but very much occupied with the teaching of forgiveness though the mode of nonviolence, thus forming the bulwark and the foundation of the Civil Rights Movement.

I am in awe of those persons, black and white, Protestant, Catholic, and Jewish, who took such a courageous stand in those dangerous and deadly days. John Lewis is a survivor of those perilous times, which he relives in his autobiography, *Walking with the Wind*. Lewis had two heroes: Martin Luther King and James Lawson. Both men inspired him, but Lawson taught and guided Lewis (and hundreds of other young people) in the ways of nonviolence. The essence of the nonviolent way of life was the capacity to forgive.

John Lewis became a staunch believer in nonviolence. His beliefs were sorely tested when he led a "sit-in" to bring about desegregation, and during the Freedom Rides in 1961 and the March on Washington in 1963, and on "Bloody Sunday" in Selma, Alabama in 1965. During those campaigns, Lewis was beaten, and once his skull was fractured.

To this very day, Lewis believes that the practice of nonviolence "is not simply a technique or a tactic or a strategy or a tool to be pulled out when needed. This sense of love, this sense of peace, the capacity for compassion, is something you carry inside yourself every waking minute of the day."

John Lewis is now the representative for the 5th U.S. Congressional District of Georgia. He is a congressman who believes nonviolence needs to be taught nationwide, and that on the federal level a Secretary of Peace is a good idea.

I think it is a good idea to individually and collectively embrace nonviolence, forgiveness and peace as worthy New Year's resolutions for this year and into the next millennium.

5.2

In her article two weeks after noting forgiveness and nonviolence as foundational patterns of those who pursue the dream, Dorothy focuses on the civil rights leader whose "dream speech" galvanized the movement.

> **All dreams need to be recognized** (*Kokomo Tribune*, January 28, 1999)
> Martin Luther King Jr. elevated this remark, "I have a dream" to a higher level. King was a dreamer and it cost him his life. If you say, "I have a dream" and if you want to fulfill that dream it won't be easy. Be assured, it will cost you something. Dreamers come in all sizes, shapes and colors, from all walks of life. And there is no age requirement to be a dreamer.
>
> Mary McLeod Bethune, daughter of former slaves, was 9 years old when she dreamed of getting an education. And it happened at Miss Wilson's one room school in Mayesville, South Carolina. Later Mary McLeod Bethune dreamed of being a missionary to Africa. That dream was denied by the Mission Board of Moody Bible Institute of Chicago. Black people, they informed her, could not be missionaries to Africa.
>
> Recovering from that harsh rejection, Bethune moved to another dream, the dream of having her very own school. In 1904, with incredible determination and hard work, with five little girls and one dollar and fifty cents, Bethune transformed a Daytona dump site into the Educational and Industrial School for Negro Girls. Over the years, her school developed into an accredited high school and then into a college.
>
> The Board of Education of the Methodist Episcopal Church (now the United Methodist Church) also had a dream: a dream to merge their school, Cookman College, with Bethune's school to form the Bethune-Cookman College. That dream continues alive and well. Today Bethune-Cookman College, located in Daytona Beach, Florida, has an enrollment of over 2300 and offers degrees in 36 areas of study.

Recently a different dream came true for 1,500 lucky people at Evansville's Robert Stadium. They were there to hear guest speaker Yolanda King, daughter of Dr. Martin Luther king and Coretta Scott King. I wish I could have been there too! The occasion was the first annual Evansville's Ministers Wives Council Scholarship Banquet—a fund-raising event. Over $8000 was raised and 12 students received scholarships so their dreams too can become realities.

Yolanda King told the crowd, "My parents were the modern-day architects of 'The Dream.' I am a 100 percent dyed-in-the-wool believer in 'The Dream' and I choose to serve with a heart of grace and soul generated by love."

Her mother, Coretta Scott King, has seen at least two of her dreams come true that I thought were impossible dreams. The one I believed most impossible was the dream of a Martin Luther King Holiday. But, on November 2, 1983, a Republican president, Ronald Reagan, signed that dream into reality, making the third Monday in January the Martin Luther King Holiday, which began in 1986.

Mrs. King's lesser known dream was to establish the Martin Luther King Jr Center for Nonviolent Social Change (The King Center). Careful planning and dedication to this dream began June 1968. Located in Atlanta, Georgia, in a 23 acre neighborhood, The King Center is the place of Dr. King's entombment, his house, The Freedom Hall Complex and the Ebenezer Baptist Church.

In 1980 The King Center was declared a National Historic Site and it attracts thousands of visitors from around the world. Since that time, additions to the site include exhibit halls, a library and archives.

An honest look at America today reveals an America that has not yet fulfilled Martin Luther King's dream. Mrs. Coretta Scott King says, "We still must seek opportunities for reconciliation, for working together for the dreams for all Americans, and for struggling until we can all stand together and shout, 'Free at last, free at last, thank God Almighty, we're free at last.'"

5.3

In her January 2000 article Dorothy offers intimate views of how Coretta Scott King and her children dealt with Martin's death and committed themselves to the continued unfolding of the dream.

They killed the dreamer but the dream lives on (*Kokomo Tribune*, January 12, 2000)

In one of her informative long distance phone calls my Chicago friend, Henrietta, mentioned how well Martin Luther King Junior's four now-grown children were faring, particularly preacher-speaker-lawyer-author Bernice King.

This was a happy coincidence since I just recently heard Bernice King being interviewed on the Diane Rehm Show on National Public Radio. I caught the tail-end of their conversation, so I didn't hear the title of Bernice's book she was discussing with Diane. Fortunately I managed to find the book at the Kokomo-Howard County Public Library—*Hard Questions, Heart Answers* by Reverend Bernice A. King.

One of the early sentences in her book jumped out at me: "They were able to kill the dreamer but they will never kill the dream." Bernice King knows the truth of that statement as well as anyone although she is the youngest of the four offspring of Coretta Scott King and Martin Luther King Jr.

On April 9, 1968, *Ebony Magazine* photographer Moneta Sleet Jr. snapped the Pulitzer Prize winning photo of Bernice King nestled on her mother's lap in a pew at Ebenezer Baptist Church in Atlanta. The sad occasion was the funeral of her father, Dr. Martin Luther King, Jr. That poignant picture included among my Martin Luther King memorabilia always left me wondering what happened to that little girl. I am glad to know that she is alive and well, a young adult who is following her dream.

Widow Coretta Scott King and thousands upon thousands of King supporters worked tirelessly for years on their dream of getting a Martin Luther King Holiday on America's calendars to honor the slain dreamer. On November 2, 1983, President Reagan signed a bill declaring the third Monday in January to be the Martin Luther King Holiday, beginning in 1986. Opposition to this law was immediate and horrendous but the dreamers prevailed and this National Holiday found its way onto the calendars and into the lives of those willing to honor Dr. King.

Lerone Bennett Jr, an *Ebony* editor and the author of a king biography, *What Manner of Man*, was a classmate of Martin Luther King Jr. at Morehouse College. He remarked about observing the King holiday: "This is not a holiday for rest and frivolity and play. This is a day for study, struggle and preparation. . .and if we ever loved him, we will use this time to mobilize against racism, militarism, unemployment and violence."

Truly, it is a day to honor and remember the man and his message: "I have a dream that one day this nation will rise up and live out the true meaning of its creed— 'We hold these truths to be self-evident, that all men are created equal.'"

Happy Birthday, Martin!

5.4

The celebration of Martin Luther King Jr. Day in January typically prompts Dorothy also to highlight the contributions of other African American dreamers. In 2004 she features a historian, an educator who established a college, and a United Methodist bishop.

Columnist reflects on some great African Americans
(*Kokomo Tribune*, January 17, 2004)

No doubt about it, the "I have a dream speech" was the most quoted speech of the 20th century. It was the perfect speech for a perfect cause—the goal of unity that transcends race, creed or color. Martin Luther King's inspiring words motivated many people to pursue and fulfill their personal and public dreams.

Long before Martin Luther King's famous speech there lived another dreamer. He was African American Carter G. Woodson, born December 19, 1875, in

Buckingham County, Virginia, just 10 years after the Civil War ended.

Woodson's dream as a young man and until his death at age 74 in 1950 was to collect sociological and historical data on African Americans and publish it in a scholarly manner. *The Negro in our History* and *The Journal of the Negro History* were two of many books he produced.

Woodson believed that the achievements of African Americans when properly set forth reveal early as well as modern contributions to civilization. And he believed this would lead to "the promotion of harmony between the races by acquainting the one with the other."

The finishing touch of Woodson's dream was organizing Negro History Week on February 7, 1926, which was expanded in the 1960s to Black History Month.

Mary McLeod Bethune was a great African American educator and definitely a dreamer. Several times while she was asleep she dreamed about deep, wide, swift-moving rivers she had to cross. Bethune would awaken and believe the dream meant she would have huge problems to solve and tremendous challenges to face.

One early challenge she faced was leaving the cotton field and "crossing over" to the field of education in Mayesville, South Carolina. That was where 9-year-old Bethune finally got a chance to attend school for the very first time. When Bethune grew up and became a teacher, she taught at the same school she had attended as a child. Bethune also taught at a few other segregated schools.

Bethune dreamed of having her very own school. That dream came true in 1904, with determination and hard work, with five little girls and one dollar and fifty cents. In spite of huge problems to solve, Bethune transformed a Daytona dump site into her school for black girls.

Over the years, her school developed into an accredited high school and then into a college, Bethune-Cookman College. Today Bethune-Cookman College is one of the United Methodist twelve historically black colleges. Bethune-Cookman College is located in Daytona Beach, Florida, has an enrollment of more than 2300, and offers degrees in 36 major areas of study.

Is Bishop Woodie White a Hoosier dreamer? He is the first black bishop of the United Methodist Church of Indiana. He affirmed, "Only a dreamer could be born at 136 Street and Lenox Avenue (in Harlem) and become a bishop of the church."

One winter morning in 1954, in Harlem, White said "yes" to become a minister. In 1954 he was a very young man but, "I knew that's what I was supposed to do." White got the necessary training which included a Masters of Divinity Degree at Boston University in 1961. Wherever and whenever possible, White was involved in the Civil Rights movement in the 1960s.

In 1963 White was arrested and jailed in Mississippi for trying to worship at a white church. In Michigan, he was the pastor of some white churches. In 1967, during the race riots in Detroit, White and a white minister walked the streets of Detroit preaching peace.

"In every appointment I've had, I have always been the first African American to do it. That comes with considerable pressure," said White. He has been "grace under pressure" in such high profile United Methodist appointments as: the first black General Secretary of the Commission on Religion and Race (1969–1984), the first black bishop in Illinois (1984–1992), the first black bishop in Indiana (1992–2004). That "yes" in 1954 stretched into 50 years of service from Harlem to Hoosier land.

I've had the privilege of speaking to and listening to Bishop Woodie White at various church functions. Many churchgoers, to their delight, call him "the singing Bishop" because he often includes a song when he preaches.

I have observed the Bishop as he presides over the church's business at the Annual Conference. He is fair and balanced and exhibits "the patience of Job."

Bishop White will retire on August 31, 2004; Indiana's loss. He will move on to other places where his quiet strength and his expertise will be a blessing and will continue to make a difference.

5.5

A vision for full inclusion encounters barriers both locally and globally. Those who envision the victory of justice over hatred find ways for this dream to become reality at the local level. Dorothy cites several examples.

> **The slow genesis of the Carver Center** (*Kokomo Tribune*, February 4, 2002)
>
> On Saturday, January 18, 2003, big snowflakes blown by a blustery wind quickly blanketed the ground, the street, and the cars and vans parked at Carver Community Center. But inside the center there was warm welcome for the guests from Indianapolis.
>
> The most honored guest was Henry A. Perry Jr. on the occasion of his 81st birthday. A time for good food, a birthday cake with lots of candles and a taste of oral history, living history in the person of Mr. Perry. This birthday celebration was also a homecoming.
>
> Friends and family members listened with rapt attention as Perry reminisced about his younger days in Kokomo and his father's concern for and dedication to the black children and youth in the community. Perry's father, the late Rev. Henry A. Perry Sr., was the founder of Carver Community Center. He was also a minister at Wayman Chapel AME and the principal at Douglas School.
>
> The year 1929 was the year Martin Luther King was born. And that was the year Rev. Henry A. Perry Sr. had a dream: a dream to rise above Kokomo's segregation practices. He dreamed of having a place where black children and youth could go for recreation because Kokomo's parks, swimming pool and the YMCA were off-limits to them.
>
> Ten years later, the dream deferred began to take shape. Land became available and the long hard struggle of fund-raising began. It was a community-wide effort. Children, youth, the teachers of Douglas School and people in the neighborhood all took part. The young Perry sisters accompanied their father on many fund-raising trips.

There were white people too who contributed to the fun-raising efforts. Perry Jr. especially remembered Max Gerber and Hobart Barnes. Later on the city gave important financial assistance.

The Perry family and scientist George Washington Carver were close friends long before he was famous. Rev. Perry Sr., his wife, and Perry Jr. were graduates of Tuskegee Institute in Tuskegee, Alabama, where Carver taught and did his research. Rev. Perry Sr. got permission to place Carver's name on the Center. Carver died in 1943 before the Center was built. The dream was deferred again due to World War II. All activities concerning the Center stopped. Then in 1946 the fund-raising resumed and the construction of the Center began in 1947. On June 15, 1947, the Carver Community Center was dedicated.

If the late Rev. Perry Sr. were alive today I'm sure he'd be pleased with today's Carver Community Center—the improvements, the additions and the healthy transition from segregation to integration.

About 26 years ago, Millard Fuller had a dream of building decent, affordable houses for people wherever substandard housing existed. And thus Habitat for Humanity was born. Since 1976, Habitat has built or renovated 125,000 houses around the world.

Last June, Mindy Rosengarten of New York City traveled with the Jimmy Carter Work Project 2002 to Durban, South Africa to build Habitat Houses No. 901 to 1000. Mindy was chaplain at the morgue at Ground Zero in the aftermath of Sept.11, 2001. She had a piece of molten glass from Ground Zero which she packed and took with her on that trip.

To Mindy, House no. 911 at the Habitat building site in Durban seemed the perfect place for that molten piece of glass. It would symbolize "building something back up." The African home owner agreed. The molten glass was embedded in the wall by the front door underneath shiny new brass house numbers: 911.

The African home owner said, "The reason behind the stone is so important: to remember those who died.

The stone will be here in my house forever. It is my job to protect the stone and its message."

Habitat for Humanity started in Kokomo in 1990, and Bob Whitehead was involved from its beginning. There are over 20 Kokomo Habitat Homes, says Bob. And one of those Habitat families is especially happy right now because they just paid off their mortgage last month!

Habitat helps people like that family. Hard-working people who can't finance a home through the banks because they don't make enough money to be eligible for a bank loan. Habitat arranges house payment at levels these people can afford.

Clearly Rev. Perry Sr. and Millard Fuller are two men who had a lot in common: a great love for people and a deep desire to make a difference.

5.6

Several of Dorothy's articles remind her readers that Blacks are not the only ones longing for liberation and full inclusion. Long entrenched white supremacist narratives have helped European conquerors to rationalize their treatment of the indigenous people who were living on the land when they arrived as settlers. Dorothy came to realize that American history needs to be taught from the perspective of the first nations whose land has been taken from them. Should Columbus Day laud the accomplishments of the invaders or lament the plight of those who were shoved aside?

Rethinking Christopher Columbus (*Kokomo Tribune*, October 18, 1998)

Since 1992, a five masted ship has been on tour around the U.S. This ship is called the Nina, a replica of one of the ships Christopher Columbus used when he sailed to the New World in 1492.

I went to see the Nina when it docked on the Ohio River in downtown Evansville. I was amazed at its size: very small. I could not imagine where the people and the ship's cargo could fit on such a tiny vessel. It was incredible to think that such a crude frail-looking boat could survive at sea. No one can doubt Columbus' navigational skills that got him and his crew to the America and back to Spain four times.

It must have been an October day near the Columbus Day holiday when Jacqueline, a Caucasian friend, approached me with a magazine called *Rethinking Schools*. She was very upset about the special issue entitled *Rethinking Columbus*. I dutifully took the magazine from her but placed it on my growing pile of things to read. . .later.

It was many months later when I finally took a closer look at the magazine's special issue *Rethinking Columbus*. I discovered that the articles were very Pro-Native American. In one of these articles, Suzan Shown Harjo, a Cheyenne, stated that many native Americans are opposed to the October Christopher Columbus holiday. "We have no reason to celebrate an invasion that caused the demise of so many of our people. . . Too often this history is passed as romantic myth, and the uncomfortable facts about Columbus are eliminated."[2]

Uncomfortable facts like the 500 Indian slaves Columbus shipped to Spain on this second voyage, with 200 Indians dying in route. And Columbus's cruel methods of extracting gold from every man, woman, boy and girl of age 14 or older. From the Native American perspective, Columbus and those who came with him and after him were invaders, not discoverers.

For many years, I taught the Christopher Columbus story the way that my fellow teachers taught it. Then one day I met Mrs. Scott, a Native American from the Oklahoma Reservation. She became my resource person to acquaint me with Native American perspectives on how to teach about the original Americans.

I stopped using the racially insensitive "I is for Indian" card, concluding that it was no more acceptable than teaching "A is for Amish" or "J is for Jew." I stopped

2. Suzan Shown Harjo, "We have no reason to celebrate an invasion," in Rethinking Columbus, edited by Bill Bigelow and Bob Peterson, 12-13, N.p. Rethinking Schools, 2003.

talking about Native Americans as though they belonged in the past, as though they all disappeared after the "First Thanksgiving." June Sark Heinrich, former director of the Native American Committee's Indian School in Chicago pointed out that today "about 1.8 million Native Americans live in what is now the United States, many on reservations and many in cities and towns. They are in all kinds of neighborhoods and schools. They are very much a part of the modern world."[3]

Rethinking Columbus is a wake-up call that the Native American's point of view of American history is an untold story; that the Indian myths and demeaning stereotypes need to be challenged by society as a whole; that Native American intellectual and philosophical contributions to this country should be more widely acknowledged. The Congressional Resolution passed by the House and Senate in 1988 is an example of one such recognition.

The original framers of the Constitution, including most notably, George Washington and Benjamin Franklin, are known to have greatly admired the concepts of the Six Nations of the Iroquois Confederacy. The confederation of the original Thirteen Colonies into one republic was influenced by the political system developed by the Iroquois Confederacy as were many of the democratic principles which were incorporated into the Constitution itself.[4]

5.7

The inhumane treatment of aboriginal tribes by invading settlers whose path to the Americas was opened by Christopher Columbus reminds Dorothy of the all-too-frequent horrendous practice of

3. June Sark Heinrich, "What Not to Teach about Native Americans," in *Rethinking Columbus*, edited by Bill Bigelow and Bob Peterson, 32–34. N.p.: Rethinking Schools, 2003.

4. Jack Weatherford, *Indian Givers: How the Indians of the Americas Transformed the World* (New York: Fawcett Columbine, 1988), pp. 133–50.

ethnic cleansing in the 20th century. Whole populations of people in particular ethnic groups around the world have been systematically annihilated. How can this pattern of violence be reversed? Dorothy points to what small groups of committed peacemakers can do to realize the dream of world peace.

Small groups can achieve the ultimate goal (*Kokomo Tribune*, April 23, 1999)

Long ago when schools taught the old-fashioned way, George's Evil Old Grandfather Rode A Pig Home Yesterday was the way I learned to spell "geography." I don't know when geography was dropped from the curriculum for more "relevant" studies. But today, we could really use some geography plus map reading skills to answer such relevant questions as: Where is Kosovo? Serbia? Albania? Yugoslavia? Another relevant question deals with ethnic cleansing.

According to *Safire's New Political Dictionary*, ethnic cleaning is the mass murder or removal of an ethnic group from an area by another ethnic group. The phrase "ethnically clean" was first used in Yugoslav politics in an April 1987 speech by Slobodan Milosevic, then head of the Communist Party in Serbia. He was discussing efforts by ethnic Albanians to drive Serbs and Montenegrins from Kosovo, where Albanians are predominant. That was then. This is now. And Milosevic is now doing the same thing he accused the Albanians of doing.

Long ago when I attended that old-fashioned school where I learned to spell "geography" the words "ethnic cleansing" did not yet exist. So the process of pushing Native Americans off their ancestral lands was called "Indian Removal." I was an adult when I learned that the infamous "Trail of Tears" was part of that Indian Removal. Author Joan Gilbert's book *Trail of Tears across Missouri* focused on the last five Indian tribes driven off their fertile lands and forced onto lands unfit for cultivation in Oklahoma. The five tribes (nations) were the Choctaws, Cree, Seminoles, Chickasaws, and Cherokees.

Cherokees were the last tribe to leave their southeastern homelands. And because they had resisted the longest against moving, their removal by U.S. government troop was particularly brutal. The Cherokees set out in late October. Most of the people walked, dressed in summer clothing. Four months later, the survivors arrived in Oklahoma in the severe winter weather of 1839.

Cherokee historians say that more than four thousand, about one-fourth of their people, died on the trek across five states—Tennessee, Kentucky, Illinois, Missouri, and Arkansas. It was a journey of almost one thousand miles, a journey in the Cherokee language "a trail where we cried." The Trail of Tears.

No continent is free from the taint of man's inhumanity to man. Each in its own way, at some point in history, has sunk to the low level of slavery, apartheid, the holocaust, the killing fields, genocide, ethnic cleansing or some other unspeakable evil. All are guilty—Europe, Asia, Africa, North and South America, Australia; but maybe not Antarctica. I'm not sure. If only penguins could talk.

Nowadays, television is saturated with conversation about the Kosovo conflict. The program that caught my attention was "Peacemakers" on C-Span. Senator George Mitchell, the author of *Making Peace*, former White House official Peter Rodman, and Chester Crocker of the U.S. Institute of Peace were the guests.

Peter Rodman warned that the U.S. cannot be the world's police, cannot get involved militarily in every conflict, cannot put out every fire around the world. Crocker suggested that our national interest would be well served if we vigorously pursued peace as a viable alternative, using better negotiation skills, more effective mediation skills, and a commanding influence in areas of conflict resolution. Through compromise diplomacy, Senator George Mitchell played a key role in bringing about a recent peace in Northern Ireland where war had been raging for 25 years.

Is an ultimate goal of peace replacing war an untenable, pie-in-the-sky, cotton-candy sentiment? The late anthropologist Margaret Mead said, "Never doubt that a small group of thoughtful, committed citizens can change the world. In fact, it is the only thing that can."

5.8

Dorothy highlights with appreciation the progress that is being made in undoing racism at Goshen College, where she attended in the 1950s.

Goshen College confronting racism (*Kokomo Tribune*, 2000)

I never ever expected to have a one-on-one, up close and personal conversation with a president. But it happened last year in October.

It was an honor and privilege to meet and talk with the President, such a charming, compassionate, intelligent person! I immediately realized how very fortunate they were—the faculty, staff, students and alumni of Goshen College—to have President Shirley Hershey Showalter as their leader.

In 1997, President Shirley became Goshen College's first woman president. She is a Mennonite (not to be confused with Amish) and Goshen College is a Mennonite college.

On the day of her inauguration, this new president made visible her advocacy and strong commitment to GC's diverse, multicultural student body as flags of 36 nations filled the room representing the 83 international students on campus. "Goshen is a biblical name," said President Shirley. "Let us be guided by the biblical imagery. . .people from all nations streaming toward the throne."

Last month on February 1, Dr. Herma Williams, a member of the Council for Christians Colleges and Universities presented President Shirley and Vice President for Multicultural Education, Zenebe Abebe, the "Racial Harmony" award.

More than 70 member schools sent letters to the CCCU regarding race relations on their campuses and their efforts toward racial harmony. Dr. Williams said, "Goshen College deserves this award. Your letter said Goshen College is serious about confronting racism, first on your campus and then in the world."

Goshen College is the only CCCU member that has a vice president for multicultural education. GC is involved in the Damascus Road anti-racism training, the Overground Railroad project, and sponsors Alumni Scholar forums to hear stories and experiences of ALANA (African, Latino, Asia, Native American) or international alumni.

I understand why GC won. The campus atmosphere and old attitudes have radically changed and improved. I saw ample evidence of this when I came on campus to speak at the Alumni Scholar Forum in October of 1999.

That same October, near Baltimore, MD, Enolia McMillan (Ms. Mac) was turning 95 years old. At age 65, in 1969, Ms. Mac became president of the Baltimore Chapter of the National Association for the Advancement of Colored People (NAACP). Then at age 80 she was elected the first woman president of the national NAACP.

Under her leadership many historic and crucial decisions were made that strengthened and improved the organization. Her knowledge, wisdom and ideas were invaluable. At age 90, she cast the decisive vote making Myrlie Evers-Williams the second woman president of the national NAACP.

Ms. Mac and President Shirley both having reached the lofty heights of the presidency, still remain teachers at heart.

Long before Ms. Mac was a local or national president, this life-long civil rights worker was an educator. She was the first black administrator assigned to an integrated school in Baltimore and she was active in the Maryland Public Schools for 42 years. "It is my role as a teacher that I have most enjoyed. When I look back on it all, I consider myself a teacher, an educator."

President Shirley echoes that same sentiment. While still a college professor at GC she promised a roomful of students that she would continue to teach. "I'm glad I made the promise to teach. In fact, I'm going to do it again next year."

5.9

Dorothy also celebrates grass roots efforts to respond to the acts of terrorism on September 11, 2001. Quilts witnessed to the power of love as a force for peace. A quilt entitled "New York City at Night" was handcrafted in time for the annual Michiana Relief Sale in Goshen. It was sold by auction on September 22, 2001 and shipped to New York to be displayed in the mayor's office as a symbol of hope.

I share an additional note about this article. At care homes where Dorothy lived during her final years we provided copies of this article to the caregivers. We did so as a reminder that when Dorothy was well she was an articulate and compassionate advocate for the way of peace and justice. We realized anew that professionals who minister to the needs of elders with dementia need to be introduced to the earlier lives of the persons in their custody.

> **Goshen wall hanging in NYC mayor's office** (*Kokomo Tribune*, October 23, 2001)
>
> The weather was just right on Saturday, September 22—a mild temperature and a bright sunny sky. Great weather for the 34th annual Mennonite Sale Day at Elkhart County 4-H Fairgrounds in Goshen, Indiana. Sale Day began at 6 a.m. with breakfast in several buildings and a wide selection of breakfast choices. There were many things to eat and see and do that day. I wanted to watch The Main Event—The Quilt Auction.
>
> There were more than 300 quilts, comforters and wall hangings to be auctioned off, with all the money going to the Mennonite Central Committee, a relief and service agency. MCC uses the money to fund programs that help the hungry, homeless, sick, illiterate, jobless, handicapped and people in war-torn situations.
>
> Each quilt, comforter and wall hanging was a stitched masterpiece, "a thing of beauty." A very special item was scheduled to be auctioned at noon, thanks to Frances Stauffer of Goshen. Frances, an 89-year old prolific quilter had a wall hanging pattern called "New York City at Night." Months ago, she had pieced together six blocks of that pattern and then set them aside to work on other quilting projects.

When disaster struck New York City on September 11, Frances remembered the unfinished wall hanging. She talked to her Quilt Committee and they decided to put the wall hanging together in time for the quilt auction. In less than three days, Frances and her committee finished the hand-quilted "New York City at Night," had it fitted in a picture frame, and ready by noon on September 22! The wall hanging went for $9000! And "New York City at Night" was shipped to New York City to hang in the mayor's office.

Some "non-quilters" from Goshen College were also at the Fairgrounds to express their concerns about the New York City and Washington disasters. College students had produced a letter stating their response to September 11. Goshen College student Heather Murphy gave me a copy.

In part it read, "We commit ourselves to not scapegoating people who have done nothing wrong. . . We commit ourselves to working for lasting peace. . . May God grant us the wisdom and courage and patience to choose creative, life-giving responses."

Mennonite Central Committee responded immediately to the New York tragedy. Mennonite Disaster Service works hand-in-hand with MCC and likewise rendered its assistance. The Federal Emergence Management Agency was so overwhelmed by the tremendous response from so many groups, organizations and volunteers it requested that no more material be sent to New York or Washington!

Respecting FEMA's request, the Mennonite agencies MCC and MDS changed their responses from material assistance to mental health assistance to the survivors, relatives, and rescue workers traumatized by the terrorist attacks. Joe Steiner, a social work professor emeritus at Syracuse (N.Y.) University, trained Mennonite Church members to help people suffering emotionally as a result of the horrendous attacks on September 11.

There are 16 Mennonite congregations in the New York City area. The Manhattan Mennonite Fellowship was the closest to "ground zero"—one block from the 14th Street police line sealing off the disaster site.

Who are the Mennonites? They are not Amish. They are more "modern" than Amish and have a lifestyle rooted in being very involved in humanitarian service for people nationally and around the world.

I PONDER. . .

In the face of ongoing racism, exclusion, and supremacist attitudes and behavior I tend to lose hope. I feel helpless, even lethargic, in the face of overwhelming crises: climate catastrophes, gun violence, mass murder, war, earthquakes, abusive law enforcement, prejudice against indigenous people groups, and the list goes on. The dream fades. As a person of privilege, now in retirement, I am tempted to retreat into the comfort of my sheltered perch.

Reading Dorothy's articles has pushed me to move beyond helplessness and lethargy.

Books available to me through the Goshen Public Library, especially recent releases displayed on the new books shelf, regularly increase my awareness of ongoing barriers that people of color continue to face. I am also impressed and uplifted by signs that the Dream lives on. An African American woman who is informed by a mission agency that blacks will not be accepted as candidates for missionary service in Africa directs her attention to education and establishes a college. The widow of the slain dreamer successfully lobbies for an annual Martin Luther King Day. People whose understanding of Columbus Day had been shaped by the prevailing perception that the Spanish explorer discovered America have their eyes opened to the fact that European invaders conquered and colonized the indigenous nations who lived there. Dorothy gives testimony to her changing perspective as a result of reading the history from the indigenous perspective.

At the risk of adding to the burden felt by so many people on the margins, I need their help. Might some of them risk inviting me to join the parade of champions who are energized by the dream that never dies?

6

Reflections
Nightmare and the Dream

I REMEMBER VIVIDLY THE time in 1999 when I visited a castle in Cape Coast, Ghana. Its history as a slaveholding fortress sent shudders up and down my spine. In my imagination I saw women and men from upcountry being herded into holding cells, where they helplessly awaited their fate. They became human cargo on slaving ships. Shackled together under squalid conditions they made the dangerous journey to the "new world." Many of them died before they arrived at their destination, and their bodies were thrown overboard. They were being forcibly and irreversibly requisitioned to meet the demand for labor in a faraway land across the sea.

I was haunted by my visit to this West African staging area on the slave trade supply route. However, I was free to walk away. I returned the next day to my short term teaching assignment at Good News Theological College and Seminary in Accra. A few weeks later I was back home with my family in Elkhart, Indiana. My memory of this experience as a weekend tourist in Ghana soon began to recede. Our neighbors and my co-workers and students at Anabaptist Mennonite Biblical Seminary were mostly white, so

I could readily avoid conversations with African Americans about their ancestral story.

During the time when I was reading the columns featured in this anthology I broadened my acquaintance with *The 1619 Project*. In its initial public release it is described as "an ongoing initiative from *The New York Times Magazine* that began in August 2019, the 400th anniversary of the beginning of American slavery. It aims to reframe the country's history by placing the consequences of slavery and the contributions of Black Americans at the very center of our national narrative."[1]

The gut-wrenching mental image of twenty to thirty enslaved Africans being off-loaded from the *White Lion* at Point Comfort, Virginia in August 1619 lingers in my mind. This was just the first installment of many such shiploads of people whose weeks of misery afloat on the Atlantic en route to America ushered them into the unspeakable horror of enslavement in a land they had not chosen. This massive human trafficking enterprise continued over a period of more than 200 years.

The year 1619 marks the beginning of an epoch of historic significance. The *New York Times* project launched in 1919 eventually resulted in a book that was released two years later. Nikole Hannah-Jones edited a multi-authored book, *The 1619 Project: A New Origin Story*.[2] Contributors to this volume describe the implications of slavery and its ongoing legacy from a wide variety of perspectives. How one is treated in schools, hospitals, courts or in neighborhood zoning decisions is often affected by whether one is white or Black.

One of the legacies of such blatant abuse has been the deeply entrenched Black/white wealth gap that continues to this day. Those who survived the hazardous journey from their homeland, and their descendants, were typically acquired by plantation

1. Nikole Hannah-Jones, "The 1619 Project," *New York Times Magazine*, August 14, 2019 (https://www.nytimes.com/interactive/2019/08/14/magazine/1619-america-slavery.html).

2. Nikole Hannah-Jones, ed., *The 1619 Project: A New Origin Story* (1st ed.; New York: One World, 2021).

owners to work in their fields. This investment by owners of plan-
tations resulted in the amassing of vast wealth, for themselves and
their heirs, at the expense of human beings that they considered
to be their property. As a white middle class educated male I have
realized anew that I am a beneficiary.

Dorothy's articles provide glimpses into the impact of segregation on African Americans like herself. Undoubtedly America's
original sin of slavery left a lingering legacy in Dorothy's ancestral
family, but her articles rarely mention it. Might this topic have
been largely avoided in family discussions of their history? Might
it be that her parents and grandparents did not have information
specific to their own ancestral story?

During my systematic reading of Dorothy's columns I frequently sensed that my research turned out to be, in some ways,
an oral history project. I was getting better acquainted with the
Dorothy Word that I first met in 2001. Her articles also opened
my eyes to how other African Americans experienced life in what
became the United States 157 years after the first slave ship arrived.
In the Declaration of Independence in 1776 the original thirteen
colonies formally claimed their liberation from British colonial
domination: "We hold these truths to be self-evident, that all men
are created equal, that they are endowed by their Creators with
certain unalienable Rights, that among these are Life, Liberty and
the pursuit of Happiness."

Ironically the freedom for which early European immigrants
fought was not granted to the people of African descent who were
living among them. Even after President Lincoln signed the Emancipation Proclamation on January 1, 1863, freedom from slavery
was slow in becoming a full reality. The nightmare still lingers.

As I conclude my attempt at recovering Dorothy's voice I
share two recollections about Dorothy as a person: her sense of
humor, and her faith.

Dorothy's sense of humor sometimes enlivens her articles in
ways that catch her readers off guard. "If only penguins could talk,"
she muses when she considers whether Antarctica ever needed to
deal with terrorists.

Some outlines of her public speeches found their way into her files, including some quotable material that she likely inserted to spark audience interest and attention. A prompt card entitled "A Lite Moment" is identified with the acronym UMW, possibly an indication that she quoted it in a speech to a group of United Methodist Women. I surmise that she was urging her hearers to keep pursuing their goals even when results seemed meagre:

> We, the willing,
> Led by the unknowing,
> Are doing the impossible
> For the ungrateful.
> We have done so much,
> For so long, with so little,
> We are now qualified to do anything
> With nothing.

Dorothy was also a person of faith. As a guest columnist for a community newspaper she did not often explicitly refer to her religious beliefs. However, columns in which she highlighted contributions by African American poets and musicians frequently mention hymn writers. One article tells the heartrending personal story underlying the hymn, "Precious Lord, take my hand." It was composed in 1932 by Thomas A. Dorsey, an African American musician, composer and evangelist. I found this article among her papers, handwritten, apparently never published:

"Precious Lord take my Hand"

"Precious Lord take my Hand" is a well-known song in many churches, black and white. It is not well known that it was written by Thomas A. Dorsey, a black man. He wrote hundreds of Christian songs, but "Precious Lord take my hand" is widely considered to be his masterpiece.

A long time ago, African American Christian songwriters like Dorsey had to visit black churches after worship to introduce and sell their songs. Then Dorsey had Mahalia Jackson sing his songs so the people could hear what they sound like.

One day while traveling out of town to visit some more black churches, his house caught on fire and his wife and only child died. One week later, Dorsey wrote the song, "Precious Lord, take my hand." Dorsey said that it was the easiest song he ever wrote because God gave him the words and he just wrote them down:

Precious Lord, take my hand, lead me on, help me stand,
I am tired, I am weak, I am worn.
Through the storm, through the night, lead me on to the light.
Take my hand, precious Lord, lead me home.

For a bulletin that we prepared for the graveside service Lillian did a search of Dorothy's file of informal jottings and casual notes. Under the caption "A Word from Dorothy" we included one of her significant Scripture texts:

Though I walk in the midst of trouble, you preserve me against the wrath of my enemies.
You stretch out your hand and your right hand delivers me.
The Lord will fulfill his purpose for me.
Your steadfast love, O Lord, endures forever.
Do not forsake the work of your hands.
(Psalm 138:7–8)

This hymn and this Psalm give voice to both lament and fervent trust. Dorothy lamented the brokenness, but she also trusted the dynamic impulse, the arc of the universe, that bends toward justice.

Though the nightmare lingers, the dream lives on. And the cheering section exhorts activists to continue striving for this dream to be become reality.

Printed in the USA
CPSIA information can be obtained
at www.ICGtesting.com
JSHW011231101023
49727JS00004B/14